Writing Implements and Accessories

The correct posture for writing, together with the necessary implements ready to hand. An engraved plate from Paillasson's 'L'Art d'écrire' (1783)

Writing Implements and Accessories

From the Roman Stylus to the Typewriter

Joyce Irene Whalley

GALE RESEARCH COMPANY
BOOK TOWER, DETROIT, MICHIGAN
1975

For M. and D., and P. and M.

First published in 1975 in the United States
by the Gale Research Company, Book Tower, Detroit,
Michigan 48226

Library of Congress Catalog Card Number 75-7563
ISBN 0-8103-2017-7

Printed in Great Britain

Contents

Introduction

Have you seen a child draw pictures on new-washed sand? Or graffiti scrawled on a dirty window? Or a dusty car bearing the words 'wash me'? If you have, you will have some idea of the possible beginnings of the written word. The idea of writing may have been first conceived when primitive man, dragging a branch behind him, noticed the pattern made in the dust, or by water trickling down a cave wall. This book is concerned primarily with the instruments man developed to make his primitive marks more easily transmitted. It also explores the use he made of these 'marks' as a means of silent communication as the development of language and thought progressed.

The first need of such communication is a surface on which to make marks and the second, an instrument with which to make them. A sharp twig or stone may have served primitive communities well enough but this book deals with more sophisticated societies ranging from the late Roman Empire to modern times, particularly in the western world. The desire to communicate in writing, even in this day of the telephone and radio, has still not passed away. Neither has the need to do so by hand been super-

6

seded by the typewriter or any other mechanical means yet devised. Writing is still one of the essential 'three Rs' taught in school – although it is possible that children alive today may see the end of that particular 'R'.

Everyone at some time has to handle a pen, even if only to sign his name. The 'pen' of today *may* be a fountain pen, but it is much more likely to be a version of the ball-point pen, which, since World War II, has swept all other forms aside in much the same way that the steel pen swept away the quill just over a hundred years ago. For those who wish to use the old-fashioned pen-and-nib method of writing the choice is limited, even compared with forty years ago. The need for traditional inks is kept alive only by the fountain pen user and the artist or designer.

Yet so imperceptibly has this revolution crept upon us that few have been consciously aware of it at all. When did you last buy a bottle of ink? If you are young, you may never have bought one at all. By contrast the older reader will recall the schoolroom desk of his youth, with its little round hole at the top right-hand side for the inkwell, and the disappointment he felt at not being allowed to use a

A typical nineteenth-century schoolroom equipped for a writing lesson. From 'A Manual of Writing Founded on Mulhauser's Method of Teaching Writing and Adapted to English Use', issued for schools under the Committee of the Council on Education in 1844.

fountain pen in school exercises. This indicates how rapidly an unimportant change can lead to the complete disappearance of all the items associated with the old way of doing things. Let us look at the schoolroom of the 1930s – not *so* long ago after all. A child's main equipment then would have consisted of a wooden penholder to which a steel pen nib could be fitted. The nib may have been scratchy and the ink may have flowed unevenly, but such a pen certainly made a very useful dart – something scarcely possible with the modern ball-point! The pen needed ink. This was probably supplied in the case of schools in powder form, and when mixed with water, was issued to the pupil in quantities sufficient to fill the little china inkwell. This type of ink was horrid, especially if it was not properly mixed. It also had a tendency to spread where it was not wanted, running down the shaft of the pen to the fingers and dropping blots on a newly written exercise. The child therefore needed blotting paper which, in his idler moments, could also be used for unauthorised purposes. The ink, if not in powdered form, came ready-mixed in satisfying brown stone bottles, but was equally liable to spread itself. At home, the child may have used a fountain pen, possibly of the kind filled by means of a lever in one side of the 'stem'. The ink, as today, was probably contained in a small glass bottle. The child's father probably scorned the scratchy school pen and possessed a fine modern fountain pen with a screw-top filler. Being the proud possessor of a desk or bureau, he would have kept his ink, blotter, paperknife and other writing equipment in grander style.

Today all of this equipment has vanished, replaced by the ubiquitous ball-point. If there is an inkstand in the house its function is probably purely decorative. The ink for the fountain pen remains in the little bottle in which it was purchased. As soon as objects of this sort go out of general use they tend to become of interest and even sometimes of value to the collector. It is often the least regarded everyday items that have the greater scarcity value. An important object, however out of date, is rarely lost sight

of or unrecorded. But the humble pen or inkpot, once the possession of almost every adult, has become quite difficult to find.

It is with all these fast-vanishing accessories of the older methods of writing that this book is concerned. Writing implements offer to the collector of any age or standing, something that has all the charm of age, the excitement of the hunt, even on occasions the pride of use, and yet can be geared to the individual pocket. You may pick up the odd penholder or ink-well at a local jumble sale for next to nothing – perhaps you even have one tucked away at home. Or you may be in a position to follow the antique market for porcelain or silver and pay thousands of pounds for a true collector's piece. It does not matter. Whatever your price range, there is something among the writing implements for you. Moreover, you can, if you wish, make practical use of your collection – nibs and ink which will suit many old pens are still made. At the same time you can enjoy the pleasure of owning objects that were once in constant use. A collection of writing implements and accessories is easily stored and can be attractively

'A suite of things for the Writing Table, in plain ormolu, set with corals, and producing a very elegant and pleasing effect': this was one of the luxury exhibits by Asprey's of Bond Street, London, at the 1862 International Exhibition.

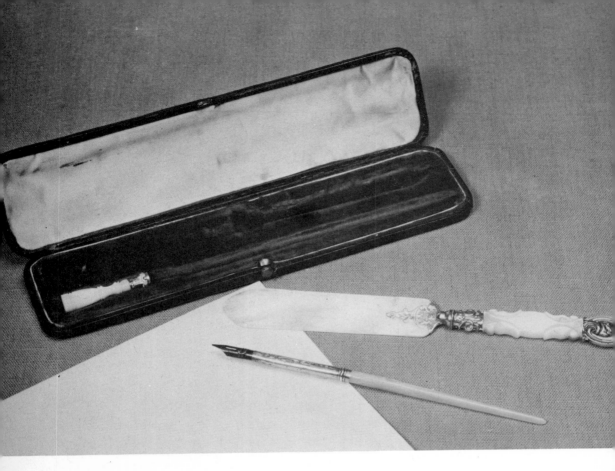

A decorative late Victorian writing set (1897) made in mother-of-pearl with silver mounts. It consists of a paper-knife, pen, and seal. Victoria & Albert Museum, London.

displayed. If you go for items at the more expensive end of the market, the silver inkstand, bronze pounce pot, or inlaid writing desk will be a part of the furniture or decoration of your home.

Apart from the traditional items, the development of the mechanical contrivance invented to lessen the manual labour of writing will be dealt with. To acquire a vintage typewriter, repair and set it to work again, may well appeal to the collector for whom the silver inkstand holds no charm.

1 The Quill Pen

Scratching marks on a rock or on a sandy, or dusty
floor may have been the earliest form of writing but
it was certainly not a convenient way of communicat-
ing. In dealing with writing implements, it is necessary to glance very briefly at the development and
history of writing. Among ancient civilisations there
were two different types of written communication.
In Egypt, letters were inscribed with a brush on
rocks or walls. They were also written with a reed
pen on papyrus sheets made from the reed which
grew so plentifully there. The latter method was
obviously the one used for business and administrative purposes. Thanks to the dry climate of Egypt,
many examples of this early form of writing have
survived to the present day, unaffected by rain or
damp. The technique can be seen clearly in contemporary wall paintings and on scrolls, giving us a
very good idea of the tools an Egyptian scribe used.
But the same conditions did not exist throughout the
ancient world. The civilisations of the Mesopotamian
plain made use of their local materials to provide a
different kind of writing from the hieroglyphics of
Egypt. This was cuneiform script – a wedge-shaped

Writing tablets, ivory, German (Cologne) 1360–70. The waxed leaves, for use with a stylus, can be seen hinged to the carved covers. Victoria & Albert Museum, London (804-1891)

This French illumination of St John (c 1400) writing with a quill is typical of the pictures which appeared in medieval manuscripts of the Gospels. Victoria & Albert Museum, London (L. 1646-1902; Reid MS 4) (photo: Courtauld Institute of Art, London)

letter-form which was impressed with an edged tool on soft clay tablets. These were then baked hard. Many such tablets from the great empires of Babylon and Assyria have survived in the soil and can be seen today in museums throughout the world. But neither Egyptian hieroglyphics nor Middle Eastern cuneiform tablets are the origin of our western writing, as we shall see in the next paragraph.

The formal Egyptian 'picture writing' was hardly suitable for everyday usage. Gradually a faster and more stylised form of signs developed, executed with a reed pen on papyrus. The Romans also used a reed pen on papyrus which they imported for the most part from Egypt. As it was not always convenient to carry pieces of papyrus around for casual jottings another method of writing existed. This was done on tablets coated with wax. Letters were incised on the waxed surface with a sharp-pointed tool called a stylus. Wax tablets were easily portable and at a time when writing material was expensive, they had an advantage in that the wax could be easily smoothed over and made ready for more writing. Illustrations of scribes, and ordinary people, using the stylus and tablets, can still be seen in Roman wall paintings and elsewhere. The stylus has remained in use for certain forms of writing throughout the centuries and waxed tablets similar to those of the Romans can be found in use in later times. They were the forerunner of the schoolboy's slate and were in fact used by the Roman schoolboy for his exercises. We tend to forget that the comparative

ginti duas esse lras apud he
breos syroru quoqz ligua z chal
deoru testatur: q hebree mag
na ex parte confinis ē. Jnā et
ꞇꞟi viginti duo elementa ſ Ꝉ

cheapness of writing paper is only recent and that for centuries any material on which people wrote was very costly, so that even the smallest scrap of papyrus, paper, or vellum was carefully used – and perhaps even used again. It was certainly not possible to waste such precious material on rough jottings or idle scribbles.

Although Roman writing tools have survived in many areas, the exact extent of literacy in the Roman Empire is uncertain. But with the gradual decline of Roman power and increased invasions along the Empire's widespread borders by peoples lacking their meticulous administrative ability, what literacy there was decayed. Throughout the so-called 'Dark Ages' Europe was in turmoil and it was not a time for the pen, but rather for the sword. Throughout the continent the church alone kept alive the lamp of learning; sometimes flickering, sometimes fading out under Barbarian invasions, but never completely extinguished. The habit of writing, together with the tools bequeathed by Roman culture, survived in the monasteries. The

A selection of writing equipment. From 'L'Art d'écrire' (1783)

15

Christian church encouraged the writing out of its sacred texts, so that its doctrine should reach as many people as possible. The importance of the scribe in a medieval monastery grew. Strange contorted pictures at the beginning of the Gospels showing the Evangelists at work began to appear in manuscripts. The portrayals varied considerably. Sometimes the saint was clasping a book, while at other times he was seen receiving inspiration from an angel or from his symbol (the angel for St Matthew, the lion for St Mark, the bull for St Luke, and the eagle for St John). But usually the writers of the Gospels were seen hard at work at their desks, pen in hand. Later these pictures came to be supplemented by illustrations of St Jerome in his study, placed at the beginning of the Bible. Such illustrations are invaluable since they provide a continuous representation of contemporary writing implements through the centuries. The early ones may appear crude and distorted, but the pens, the inkwells, the penknives, and the desks are clearly portrayed.

The pen used in these pictures of the saints was the quill pen. This was to remain the instrument used by nearly all writers, professional or amateur, from the early medieval period until just over a hundred years ago. The quill pen was made from one of the primary feathers taken from the wing of a bird – preferably a goose, but sometimes a raven, turkey, or swan. The reason for using a bird's feather was largely governed by its availability in the various European countries. But its flexibility was an important factor and it could be sharpened to such a point that quite small writing was possible – an effect less easy to achieve with the stiffer reed – and yet the edge was not sharp enough to pierce the writing surface. The actual material on which the quill was used naturally affected the shape of the writing edge, in the same way that the development of script affected the way in which the quill was cut. A study of the history of handwriting shows that it followed the stylistic trends of the day. For example, the Carolingian and Romanesque hands were rounded like the arches of contemporary churches, while the

Gothic script was pointed and angular; the early humanist hands reverted to a form of the Carolingian script in which many a classical text had been transmitted. To make the change in the letter forms it was necessary to alter slightly the angle made to the writing surface by the 'nib' or writing edge of the quill.

The earlier writing manuals of the sixteenth century were engraved on wood, but as copperplate engraving began to replace the wood-engraved copybook, the form of writing changed and with it the type of nib point. The engraver working on a copper plate could make fine hairlines and elaborate flourishes which were hardly possible on the less easily worked wood. The copperplate hand became almost over-refined, and the pupil now began to imitate the result of the graver (or 'burin') on copper. Before it was the engraver who had reproduced the style of the writing master's copy. It was the graver not the pen which affected the round handwriting of the late seventeenth and eighteenth centuries. When the steel pen nib was developed, it was able to follow the copperplate pattern with ease. But if the nineteenth-century scribe tried to imitate medieval writing with a quill, he did not succeed because he was using the quill wrongly and had a nib shaped more for contemporary writing than for medieval letter forms. The medieval quill nib shape was quite different from that of the nineteenth-century steel nib and it was not until Edward Johnston, a twentieth-century calligrapher, solved the problem of what the medieval quill had really been like that the old scripts could be copied accurately.

The remarkable thing about the quill pen was that it changed so little over the centuries: the *angle* of the nib may have varied; the *feathers* may have been goose, turkey, or even crow; the *position* of the chosen feather may have differed – nevertheless, the instrument which we see held by the early Evangelists was much the same as that portrayed in illustrations showing later writers. It was not that scribes were too contented with their instrument to want to change it.

18

The demand for a portable pen was one of the factors that led to the development of the reservoir and fountain pen. This advertisement appeared in Pigot & Co's 'Metropolitan New Alphabetical Directory for 1827'.

On the contrary, they were well aware of its shortcomings. The need to constantly repair or mend the point which easily wore out or broke, and the fact that it had to be frequently replenished with ink, were noted by professional scribes and ordinary writers alike, and the search for the perfect pen went on for centuries.

Experiments were made from time to time to fashion the quill out of metal – a prince may have been presented with a golden or silver pen and on certain occasions, as in late sixteenth-century

England, such a pen may have been the prize in a writing competition. But although the metal pen is found so early and was quite common, especially in a portable form, in the eighteenth century, it suffered from certain apparently insuperable faults. It was liable to rust and it lacked the essential flexibility of the quill, which remained without serious competitors till about 1830. Sometimes an attempt was made to replace only the point of the quill with metal, but the same disadvantages outweighed the obvious advantages.

The word 'pen', which we associate with the complete object held in the hand, originally had a much more limited meaning: it comes from the Latin 'penna', a feather. The pointed end was the 'nib', or neb, a form which was taken over when the steel pen became common. In order to make the feather suitable for writing, a number of processes were required. Some of these were carried out by the penman himself. But with the spread of literacy following the invention of printing in the fifteenth century, 'pen-cutting' became a separate industry and can sometimes be found described in books of trades. Nevertheless, it was often more convenient for the ordinary writer to make his own quill, and instructions for doing this became a part of writing manuals.

A survey of writing ability from the early centuries of Christianity up to the invention of printing will show a considerable increase in its extent. At the beginning it was the church, and especially the monastic institutions, which preserved the arts of writing and reading. For this reason the senior administrative officials attached to the royal court were often clergymen. Indeed our word 'clerk' derives from the original supposition that anyone who could write must be a cleric. As the Middle Ages progressed, trade and business expanded and stable town life became more possible. The first people to separate from the church and require their own writing and reading facilities were the lawyers and doctors. The need to cope with the increasing complexities of general government and business administration led to the increase in the number of lay scribes or 'scriveners' – a separate body of men whose services were available to all who required them. For some people, however, it was simpler to write their own letters and keep their own accounts, and so in the later Middle Ages the non-professional writer began to emerge. The Cely and Paston letters of fifteenth-century England, for example, show how the ability to write had spread. Though the letters of these two families in the wool trade are among the best known survivals, they are not the only ones. We must not forget the amount of 'family' writing that has not survived.

For all these people, both clerical and lay, there was no alternative to the handwritten word. Anything to be read first had to be laboriously copied out. To begin with, books were copied mainly in monastic scriptoria, but gradually, with the beginning of a middle-class interest and an increased demand for more books, secular copyists became common. This was also true of the decorators, or illuminators, of books. The writing was still done with the quill pen as it always had been, and manuscript representations of scribes in the fifteenth century look little different from those of the sixth or ninth centuries.

A writing master instructing his pupil on how to use a quill, how to sharpen a quill and how to write. A vignette from George Bickham's 'The Universal Penman' (1743)

The invention of printing and its spread throughout Europe brought great changes in the field of writing as in other matters. The large body of scribes who earned their living as copyists were in danger of losing their livelihood. But the multi-

BEfore you begin to Write, be accommodated with thefe neceffary Impliments or Inftruments. (viz.) 1. A choice *Pen-knife* of Razor-metal. 2. A *Hone*, and *Sallet-Oil*, wherewith to renew the Edge of your *Knife*. 3. Store of *Quills*, round, hard and clear, the Seconds in the Wings of Geefe or Ravens. 4. Pure white, fmooth grain'd, well gum'd Paper, or a Book made of fuch, well preffed. 5. The beft *Ink* that you can poffibly procure. 6. *Gum-fandrick* beaten into Powder, fearced, and tyed up in a fine Linen-cloth, wherewith pounce your Paper. 7. A flat *Ruler* for certainty, and a round one for difpatch. 8. A fmall pair of *Compaffes*, wherewith to Rule double Lines at the firft, and to keep your Lines equi-diftant. 9. A choice *Black-lead Pen*. 10. *Indian Black-duft*, or fine Sand, to throw on Letters written in hafte. 11. A fmooth *Black Slate*, whereon to exercife the command of Hand in the expeditious producing of great Letters and Flourifhes.

All thefe Accommodations will concern;
But moft of all a willing mind to learn.

Although comparatively late in date, these instructions were no doubt much the same as those given to young scribes through-out many centuries. From 'England's Pen-man; or, Cocker's New Copy-book ... Written and Engraven by Edward Cocker' (1703)

plicity of books made possible by the new methods of production led to lowering of costs – the hand-produced book had always been an expensive item. This meant that books could reach a wider public, giving more people the opportunity of learning to read and perhaps to write. There arose a new class of writing masters or teachers, whose profession was not so much to use the pen themselves, as the old scriveners had done, but rather to teach others to use it. Certain types of writing still needed the old styles of script, so that besides teaching 'everyday' hands, the writing masters also taught various legal hands, which derived directly from the gothic lettering styles. In addition they gave instruction in italic, secretary and, later, 'round hand'.

At first the writing master passed on his skill in person to his pupils; later he may have wished to circulate copies of his work, although the public he reached in this way was limited. The answer was to publish a book of copies. This could be circulated widely, even among those who could not afford a master themselves, and at the same time the published book would establish the fame of the writing master. Many of the copybooks published in the early sixteenth century still exist. They show examples of both the writing master's skill and the methods by which he attained it.

The English copybook was strongly influenced by the earlier Italian masters who, mainly because of the importance of the scribes of the Papal chancery, led the way in writing skills. In both the Italian and English books, precise instructions on how to make and use the quill pen are frequently found. They are some of the most detailed accounts to come down to us and, allowing for personal preferences of par-

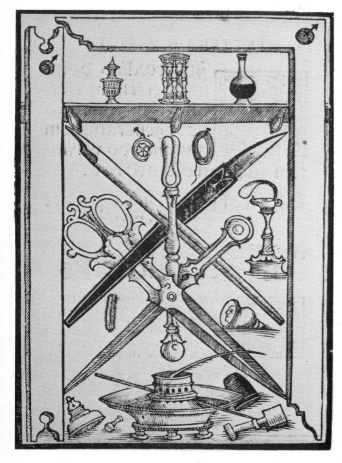

A composite picture from 'Libro nuovo d'imparare a scrivere' by Giovanni Battista Palatino (1540) showing every possible aid to the writing master's art.

ticular teachers, the general descriptions cannot differ greatly from earlier ways in which the quill had been prepared for use by generations of both clerical and lay scribes. Among the earliest of the Italian writing masters to give details about the implements of his trade was Giovanni Battista Palatino, in his *Libro nuovo d'imparare a scrivere*, 1540, which has been recently translated into English by Dr A. S. Osley. In addition to a description of all the implements needed by a scribe, Palatino included a composite picture of them, which shows us exactly what he considered necessary and what each item looked like in the first half of the sixteenth century. On the method of preparing the quill he has the following to say:

Stages in the preparation of the quill, together with a suitable pen knife. From 'Libellus valde doctus' by Urban Wyss (1549)

Quills for writing the chancery hand should be from the domestic goose, they should be hard and clear, and small rather than large, because thus they can be used with greater ease and speed. It does not matter from which wing they are taken, though some writers draw a great distinction here; those which are taken from the right wing should be broken off or bent above the barrel so that they

do not twist when held in the hand; which is a serious impediment to rapid, even writing.

Quills should be kept clean of any ink which remains after writing, because old ink interferes with the flow of fresh ink. They should invariably be kept in a vessel with just enough water to cover the part which has been cut to form the nib. A quill must never be allowed to dry out, because this makes your letters ragged and feeble, and it is extremely difficult to write with such quills. You should be careful not to rub quills with a cloth or put them under hot ashes, as many do to make them round.

Also of interest is the illustration which appears in *Libellus valde doctus* by Urban Wyss, published in Zurich in 1549. The quill is first seen almost in its natural state and then the stages by which it is converted into a usable instrument of writing are shown. This is achieved with a pen knife. This tool was a requirement at all times for the scribe and the observant reader will have noticed it appearing in some of the illustrations already seen in this book.

An illustration from 'Libellus valde doctus'. It shows various writing implements and accessories set out ready for use, among them a penner and inkpot, similar to the one shown in the illuminated manuscript on page 89.

25

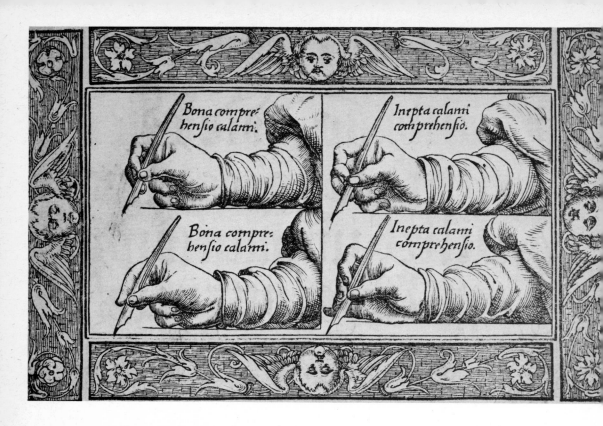

An illustration from 'Libellus valde doctus' showing the right and wrong way to hold the quill.

Also in Wyss's work is a series of illustrations on the right and wrong way to hold the pen. The final form of the nib depended to some extent on the style of the writing used but the way in which the writer held his quill also influenced its shape. There has always been, in the eyes of teachers at least, a correct way of holding a pen, though this has differed from teacher to teacher, and from century to century. Sometimes this information was given in words in the part of a copybook devoted to the verbal instruction of the pupil, but it is obvious that an illustration conveyed much more to the learner than any number of words. Similar pictures occurred frequently in various writing books, including some of the English ones. Quite often it is the same picture, repeated from book to book in identical fashion, or perhaps merely reversed in the printing, but almost always without acknowledgement to the original writing masters.

One of the earliest English writing masters was Martin Billingsley, writing master to Charles I when he was Prince of Wales, who published *The Pens Excellencie; or, the Secretaries Delighte* in 1618. He was not the first, but because of his published work he is one of the most famous. He gives detailed instruction for making a quill pen as well as for the proper method of holding it when made.

Billingsley is talking about the quill ready for use. We must look elsewhere to find an account of the method of preparing the feather straight from the bird, ready for the writer to make into a pen. One method is given in a later work, *The Dictionary of Arts and Sciences*, 1754:

> In order to harden a quill that is foft, thruft the barrel into hot afhes, ftirring it till it is foft, then taking it out, prefs it almoft flat upon your knee with the back of a penknife, and afterwards reduce it to a roundnefs with your fingers. If you have a number to harden, fet water and alum over the fire, and while it is boiling put in a handful of quills, the barrels only, for a minute, and then lay them by.

The correct way to hold the pen as shown in John Davies's 'The Writing Schoolemaster; or, the Anatomie of Faire Writing' (1648)

In the next place I hold it neceſſary to ſet downe certaine rules for the making and holding of the *Pen*, with other things thereunto appertaining.

Obſeruations or rules for the making of the Pen.

AFter you haue gotten you a good Pen-knife well edg'd and ſmooth'd vpon a hoane, and good ſecond quils, either of Gooſe or Rauen, ſcraped with the backe of your knife, begin to make your Pen thus :

1 Firſt, holding your quill the right ſide vpwards, cut off about the third part of it flat along to the end.

2 And turning it on the backe ſide, cut off the very end of it aſloape; which being done, it will be forked.

3 Then, holding it ſtill on the backe, make a little cut in the very midſt of the quill.

4 When you haue done ſo, take the end of your knife if it haue a pegg, or elſe another quill, and make a ſlit vp ſuddenly, euen in the cut you gaue before.

5 Which being done, turne your quill on the right ſide againe, and begin to cut a little thought aboue the ſlit, on that ſide which is next your left hand, and ſo continue cutting by degrees, till you thinke you haue ſufficiently cut that ſide. But herein you muſt bee very wary you cut not off too much of the ſlit; for then your pen will be too hard, and if you leaue too much alſo, it will be ouer ſoft.

6 Then euen againſt the place you beganne to cut the firſt ſide, cut the other likewiſe, till you haue made them both of an equall thinneſſe : and then trying it by lifting vp the ſlit vpon the naile of your thumbe, you ſhall ſee whether it be too ſoft or too hard : if either, bring it to a meane by adding more ſlit to it, if you ſee it be too hard; or by taking ſome away, if you perceiue it to be too ſoft.

Laſtly, herein lies the difficulty, *viz.* in the nibbing of the Pen : wherein I obſerue this rule, that placing it on the naile of my thumbe, or middle finger, I hold my knife ſomewhat ſloaping, and cut the end of the nibbe, not quite off, but before my knife come off, I turne him downe-right, and ſo cut the nibbe cleane away, on both ſides alike; contrary to that old vulgar rule, *Dextra pars penna, &c.* Now if my pen be to write full, I cut off ſo much the more of the nibbe; if ſmall, ſo much the leſſe.

[marginal note:] Note that if your quill (as many haue) haue teeth, you are to pare it on the back thinly, to take them a-way. Obſerue that this nibbing of the Pen muſt be done at once though it ſeeme two ſeuerall cuts, otherwiſe it will not write currantly.

Obſeruations for the holding of the Pen.

1 HOld your Pen betweene your thumbe, your fore-finger, and your middle-finger : *viz.* with the top of your thumbe, the bottome or lower part of your forefinger, and the toppe or vpper part of your middle finger.

2 And let your other two fingers ioyne to the reſt a little thought within them; ſuffering none of your fingers with which you hold the Pen, to touch paper: for that is the proper office of the fourth and little fingers, by which the ſtrength of the others is maintained.

3 Laſtly, for the right vſage of the Pen, when you can hold it; you ſhall obſerue, that it ought to be held directly vpon the full: for that is moſt proper, being that the nib of the Pen muſt be cut euen, otherwiſe it is ſubiect to ſpatter. Howbeit, I deny not, but in the fetching of any compaſſe, it muſt be held a little inclining to the left ſide : for ſo the Pen will giue full where it ſhould, and ſmall alſo where it is required.

Note, that the Pen muſt be held very gently in the hand, without griping, becauſe of two inconueniences which come thereby.

1 The one is, that the command of hand (which otherwiſe by the eaſie holding thereof is to be attained) is hereby vtterly loſt.

2 The other is, that by this griping, or hard holding of the Pen, a man is kept from a ſpeedy diſpatch of that he goes about to write : both which are maine enemies to Clerke-like writing.

M. B. his priuate opinion concerning Pen-manſhip.

1 FIrſt, it is a moſt abſurd and hatefull quality, to vſe any manner of botching in the Art of *Writing*; yea, though it be in a letter of the greateſt vncertainty.

2 Againe, I am of opinion, that although in the writing of ſome *Hands*,

(2

Other similar recipes for removing the unwanted substance from the original feather are given elsewhere and presumably there has been little change in methods over the centuries.

In the story of English handwriting, many descriptions of pen making, and ways of using the quill for different styles of writing, are to be found in the published works of the various writing masters. Those readers who desire to learn more about the subject are able to do so either from the original works or from the facsimiles which are issued from time to time.*

It has already been mentioned that one of the reasons why the quill superseded the reed pen was that it was more easily obtainable in the countries of western Europe. It gradually became established that on the whole the goose quill was the most satisfactory for the majority of scribal needs. Fortunately the goose was one of the most common of domestic fowls. The desire for fresh meat throughout the year led to the importance of the village duck pond and the poultry run (cattle being slaughtered during the winter when feedstuff was unavailable).

*See the works listed in Sir A. Heal, *English Writing Masters and Their Copybooks* (1931), and J. I. Whalley, *English Handwriting* 1553–1850 (1969).

Quills being plucked from geese, as illustrated in the Rev Isaac Taylor's 'Scenes of British Wealth in Produce, Manufactures, and Commerce, for the Amusement and Instruction of Little Tarry-at-home Travellers' (1823)

The goose was therefore plentiful in medieval and indeed post-medieval England and readily provided the necessary feathers. Increased demand led in time to a certain amount of specialisation and in *Scenes of British Wealth*, a book for the instruction of children by Isaac Taylor published in 1823, we find that the Lincolnshire fens were particularly famous for their geese quills. Taylor writes:

Though such numbers are seen together in these fens only, yet when it is recollected that every cottage keeps, and every green swarms with them, the number of geese in England must be very great.

This is seen in a curious way, when large flocks, of eight or ten thousand, are driven to London. A piece of red rag, on a long stick, scares them on. They travel about eight miles a-day.

But we have not done with the fens and the geese there. Their feathers and quills are so valuable, that the avarice of man has put aside his better feelings; the geese do not live in peace till they die, and know nothing more about it; but, about the end of March, they have their quill feathers pulled out to make pens, and their other feathers also.

When Isaac Taylor was writing this, experiments with a steel pen nib were already well advanced and soon only the old fashioned would continue to hanker after the instrument used throughout the centuries. As the quality of the steel pen improved it may have been thought that the end of the quill was at hand but, in fact, this was not so, and quills can still be bought today.

The reason for this has nothing to do with an unwillingness to accept modern methods, but rather a revival of interest in the crafts of an earlier day. The handwritten book was considered rather barbaric by those who rejoiced in the new-fangled method of printing, an attitude which continued among the majority of people for centuries. But a few antiquarians still found manuscripts attractive and some, like Horace Walpole, included them in their collections of 'gothick' or medieval art. The nineteenth century also saw a much more scholarly attitude to the Middle Ages and all aspects of the arts and crafts were studied with interest. Certain

OPPOSITE
Enlarged detail from the Diepenveen Bible showing a monastic scribe sharpening his quill with a pen knife. Netherlandish 1450-3. Victoria & Albert Museum, London. (L. 1663-1902; Reid MS 23) (photo: Courtauld Institute of Art, London).

artist-scholars, among them men like Henry Shaw, Noel Humphreys, and Owen Jones, collected manuscripts themselves or studied them in places like the British Museum. They also attempted to copy what they saw and published the results for the benefit of others. The invention of a commercially viable method of colour printing in the second half of the nineteenth century assisted the spread of this interest in medieval manuscripts and in the methods of their production. Manuals for amateur illuminators were issued in large numbers. Among those who attempted to produce modern versions of the medieval illuminated manuscript was that great supporter of hand-produced craftwork, William Morris.

It was Edward Johnston (1872–1944) who led the way back to the traditional use of the quill. He realised that the quill, which was used to form the letters of the medieval manuscripts in which he was interested, was cut with a broad sloping nib which made the letter form without any further manipulation of the pen – a fact which earlier calligraphers had not appreciated. Johnston and his followers taught calligraphy as a subject in art schools and their example was followed elsewhere. It coincided with a revived interest in letter-forms which expressed itself in the productions of the private presses. This led to a renewed demand for the quill pen – not great, but continuing. Today, quills can be bought in the sort of shops that supply artists' materials and they are still used, together with the reed pen, for manuscript work. Rolls of honour, presentation scrolls and similar items are still written out in the age-old method using the traditional tools, though the style of writing may be entirely in the modern idiom. Once again 'how to do it' books proliferate, sometimes containing instruction on how to prepare your own quill, but nowadays such methods are used from choice and not from lack of an alternative. In England, a professional body of scribes exists, many of them members of the Society of Scribes and Illuminators, which recently celebrated its half-century. The goose feather pen is unlikely to disappear in this century at least.

The Pen Knife and Quill Cutter

Without the pen knife there could be no good quill.
The knife, next to the pen, was one of the most
important tools for the scribe. Knives are items which
are taken so much for granted that we fail to
appreciate their importance to our ancestors, when
the possession of a good knife – handmade of course –
was a matter of great concern. The poorer people
possessed only one knife which was made to perform
all kinds of tasks for which there are now a variety of
shapes and sizes. This included its use as a food knife.
One might almost say that in addition to taking the
place of a fork (before its invention) it sometimes
even took the place of the spoon too, since there are
frequent warnings in the 'courtesy' books of the
Middle Ages that it should *not* be used in this way in
company. But the everyday, all-purpose knife was
not the one recommended to the professional scribe.
Its importance to him can be deduced by the fact
that nearly every illustration of an evangelist,
St Jerome, or other writer in action, shows a pen
clutched in one hand and in the other something
that sometimes looks like another pen, but which is
in fact his knife.

The scribal knife served two purposes. It was used as an eraser of writing faults and it mended the pen. A careful scribe would perhaps keep two separate instruments, but for the most part, the one knife served both purposes. The knife-eraser was essential before the invention of india rubber and other methods of deletion. The early scribe was writing on vellum, a much tougher material than paper and one which would stand up to the knife treatment more easily. Certain kinds of ink which did not sink into the writing surface could in fact be gently scraped off. A sharp tool can still be effective today. But the proper preparation of a scribe's pen was even more important. The exact description of the pen knife appeared much later than its illustration in manuscripts, but combining pictorial evidence and the words of later scribes we can get a good idea of its shape, size and method of employment. Obviously such a knife would have to have been quite small and easily held in the hand. It would have needed a good point and blade, suited to the work it had to do in preparing the nib for writing. The quill as it was probably received by the scribe – with its feather part trimmed and excess grease etc removed – still needed a lot of attention. It did not in the least resemble an instrument for writing and had to be pared to something approaching a point, then slit for flexibility, and finally the actual writing edge had to be shaped to suit the user and the style of writing – a simple sharp point was not only scratchy to use but penetrated the writing surface. Once made, the point or nib needed frequent renewal as it quickly wore with use. To prevent the blade of the knife from either receiving or causing damage, it was provided with a sheath. In the Middle Ages this would probably have been of leather, later it may have been of some other suitable material, though leather always remained popular. Although the knife was an essential tool for all writers and therefore a thing in common use, it also lent itself to decoration. While the handle and sheath of an everyday pen knife were often quite unadorned, others were richly decorated and even ornamented

34

with semiprecious stones. For purely practical reasons the blade needed to be of steel, even for the pen knives of princes, but the haft and sheath could be made to suit the whim and purse of the owner or donor. Pen knives are therefore very attractive objects to collect and although one cannot hope to have many of those made in more precious materials, one or two with silver, ivory or mother-of-pearl handles enhance any collection. As in so many instances, it is the more humble object that is difficult to acquire – the simple everyday unadorned tool which was used till it wore out and then discarded – but from time to time they do appear on the market.

One of the early printed descriptions of the pen knife appears in the Palatino work, quoted earlier, and given here in Dr Osley's translation:

> The knife for cutting the quills should be of good steel, well-tempered and well-ground. It should be pointed. The handle must be rather sturdy and

A selection of pen knives: an engraved plate from 'L'Art d'écrire'.

square so that it does not twist about in your hand when you are using it. It should be three times as long as the blade, though it can be more or less, depending on the length of the blade, provided that it is comfortable and can be firmly held. The blade should be rigid & not hollowed. It should curve a little forward [see the illustration on page 23]. The back should be square, not round, with somewhat sharp edges so that you can scrape the quill. Do not use it to cut paper or hard substances that blunt the edge, but keep it exclusively for the job of cutting your quills.

Edward Cocker, writing in *The Pens Perfection* in 1672, gives instructions for keeping the tool in good condition, and tells how to obtain a good working instrument:

> Neither the Cuttler, nor the Mark can warrant a Pen-Knife good, for though the best Workman commonly performes the best Work, yet the most Exquisite cannot always hit the most excellent Temper. He marks them all alike, let them prove how they will. The best are to be found amongst those made of Razer Metall; which are wrought down from a thick Back to a curious thin Edge; which being tried by use is best recovered by running of it gently over a fine Hone with Sallet Oyl, and afterwards smoothed on the rough side of a Thong of Neats Leather or the top of your Shoe. You may best set an Edge on a common Pen-Knife, with a fine gritted Whetstone and Water. Whet not your Pen-Knife cross over Blade, but draw it sidewayes over the Hone or Stone, so will the Edge quickly come to perfection with less prejudice to the Blade.

In spite of technical improvements, the best kind of pen knife remained elusive. Writing in *The Technical Repository* for 1827 the editor has much to say on the continuing difficulty of getting a suitable knife:

> Our readers would in vain seek to find amongst the cutlers, a knife suited to the purpose of pen-cutting; nor, indeed, do any of the many treaties on that useful art afford any information, on the peculiar shape given by the pen-cutters themselves to their knives.

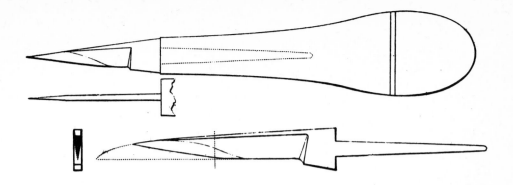

Having often had occasion to experience the excellence of the pens made and mended for the use of the members of the Society of Arts, &c.&c., the Editor enquired after the pen-cutter,* and on learning his residence called upon him. He found him and several of his family engaged in pen-cutting, and could not but remark the peculiar form of their knives. On questioning him upon the subject, he very readily gave the Editor all the information in his power, and told him that he never could get the cutlers to shape their knife blades in such a manner as to be at all fit for his use; and that he had to labour for a considerable time upon every new blade before he could bring it to a proper form. This may possibly be owing to the small price, sixpence each, which the cutlers charge for the pen-cutters' knife blades; but we cannot but think, that if they would study the pen-cutters' convenience, and shape their blades so as to please them, which they could have no difficulty in doing, the pen-cutters would be glad to be spared so much trouble, and afford a higher price accordingly.

As it is, the pen-cutters have, as we above state, to shape their knives themselves. Fig 3 [above] represents a blade, the form of which, as made and sold by one of their favourite cutlers, Mr. Smith of Cheapside, is shown by the dotted lines; before they can use it, however, they have to alter its form in the manner shown, having previously mounted it into a round hard-wood haft, of the shape exhibited in fig 4, by means of cement.

* Mr. Cotmore, Stangate, Lambeth

The shaping of a quill cutter as described in a passage in 'The Technical Repository' (1827)

Mr. Cotmore said that he first whetted it into shape upon a Turkey stone with oil, (possibly, however, he first employs a grindstone to bring it nearer to his form), laying it flat upon the stone, with his finger upon it, and whetting both sides equally aslope, the point being made very sharp and slender, and the sides of it slightly rounded; the section fig 5 which is taken at the dotted line in fig 3 will, however, afford a better idea of its form. He finishes it, and renews its edge continually, whilst using it, upon a dry water of Ayr stone, and which produces a fine smooth edge, observing to give the last stroke with the back of the knife turned from him, so as to throw the edge into the right direction for cutting to the best advantage. The cast steel which the blades are made of, requires to be of a good quality; and Mr. Smith, who is a native of Sheffield, informed us that he tempers them only to a straw colour.

The pen-cutters generally work with the assistance of spectacles, which magnify somewhat considerably, in order that they may see better to give their pens their proper cut. They, after giving the quills the two first cuts, slit them a little with the slender point of the knife, the edge being held upwards, and open the slit by inserting the small conical end of another quill, held between the fingers of the right hand; and, after shaping the sides and point of the pen properly, also nib it upon that quill, into which they usually put a piece of slate pencil, in order to give it more stiffness and darken its colour, that they may see to nib the pen the more clearly. Fig 4 represents a knife in our possession, which has been in use for some time, but is yet in a good state.

The date at which this passage occurs is significant. Before the next decade was out, the steel pen nib, which needed no such attendant knife, was already being made in quantity.

I have purposely written 'pen knife' as two words, to distinguish it from the penknife as we know it today. This small useful pocket knife did not so much die as become transformed. Pencils still needed sharpening, and the pocket knife was found to have many uses never intended by the makers of the quill pen knife. So there are still penknives today, rarely

now with a decorative sheath, but usually folding in upon themselves (as indeed did some of the earlier pen knives), and often consisting of more than one blade. Using the word today, most people have never reflected that the handy little object in their pocket was indeed once a *pen* knife.

Needless to say, with the pen knife in such great demand for making quills, there were attempts to produce an instrument that would take some of the labour out of the production of a suitable writing

Gilt brass quill cutter and knife. Stamped with the maker's mark, it dates from the eighteenth century. Victoria & Albert Museum, London (M. 418-1936)

A pen and pencil case, with a pen knife, c 1870–80.

instrument. This led to the invention of several kinds of quill cutters – tools which in themselves performed the various actions otherwise done by knife and hand. The basic requirements of such a tool were that it should be able to shape the quill, slit it, and make the point for writing. A small brass quill cutter in the Victoria and Albert Museum is worked by a key or tap at the top. The quill nib is inserted in the hole provided and a turn of the highly elaborate key brings the cutting tool down on to the inserted nib. A more common form of quill cutter was the folding pocket one which looked something like a modern penknife. This provided a space at one end into which the quill could be inserted, while the shutting down of a previously raised 'arm' acted like a guillotine in shaving off the unwanted parts of the quill. A small sharp edge was also provided to cut the point of the nib, and in some cases a slim blade was concealed within the tool which could be slid out for any further trimming that was required. These pocket quill cutters appear on the market from time to time and if the slim blade has not already been broken off, may be taken for some kind of penknife – which of course they were. But a careful examination of both ends of the instrument will often show the nib-shaped cutter at one end.

The Steel Pen

Anyone who used the quill for very long inevitably became aware of its disadvantages. The carefully made point soon wore down. The nib needed frequent renewal of ink. The quill itself was but a frail item and had to be replaced if used a great deal. It was not surprising therefore that for purely practical reasons many attempts should have been made to find a better writing implement. A feather plucked from a bird is at best a humble instrument. It is not surprising that the first efforts at improvement should have concentrated on supplying princely penmen with something grander in silver or gold to replace the traditional feather quill. We therefore find pens of metal from at least the sixteenth century, and no doubt, experiments had been made before that time. Certainly there is record of a contest between Peter Bales and Daniel Johnston in 1595, the prize to be a golden pen. But the golden pen can have been a trophy only, since even a pen of gold would have suffered from the same trouble that beset any other metal pen during the experimental period – it was not flexible.

If you try to write a good hand with, for example,

PEN AND PENCIL CASES.

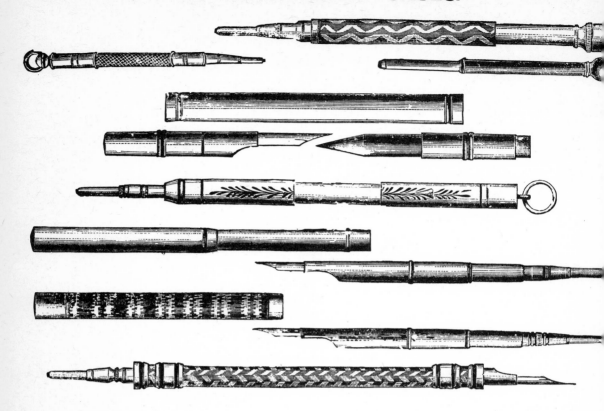

PURE NICKELLED & METAL COMBINATION POCKET PEN & PENCIL CASES

A variety of 'combination' cases available towards the end of the nineteenth century. All the pens were of course 'dip' pens, and they indicate the need for a pocket pen which would have the ink readily available when required – hence the many efforts to perfect the fountain pen.

a knitting needle or even a piece of metal more nearly adapted to pen form, you will have a good idea of the problem facing the would-be pen-improvers. Moreover, as the style of writing changed, the flexibility of the pen became more, rather than less, important – the 'thick and thin' strokes of the typical late eighteenth or nineteenth-century English round-hand needed a particularly adaptable nib. In addition to the lack of flexibility provided by the early metal pens, there was also the problem of corrosion. The ink acted on metal in such a way as to make the nib rapidly unusable. Thus either the metal needed special treatment or else the ink had to be of different composition. But the various disadvantages did not stop pens being manufactured in a variety of materials. To some of these experimental types a quill nib was fitted, while to others a metal nib similar in shape to the quill was fixed. Among the most charming of the early metal pens to survive are those found in portable writing sets. Probably never really meant for long or serious writing, they made attractive gifts and were very suitable for decoration, suggesting that they were meant for the boudoir rather than the study. For surely the writers of those interminable eighteenth- and early nineteenth-century correspondences would have taken to the quill when they settled down to write a long letter and saved the decorative toy for show, or for a signature only.

The development of the steel pen and its gradual rise to almost universal use in a period of less than fifty years was a remarkable feat in view of the long established reign of the quill. The original maker of the first steel pen will probably never be known though the claim of several artisans has been put forward. The manufacture of such pens for general sale, however, is considered to have taken place about 1829. At this date the hand-made pens were superseded by those made by 'presses' and other tools in common use in the manufacturing processes of similar small items in Birmingham. It was the general improvement of these processes, coupled with the development of methods of mass-production, which promoted the wider acceptance of the steel pen. By these mechanical means the cost of the new type of pen was gradually reduced, while at the same time the uniformity of its shape and quality was assured. Like all new inventions, the steel pen was not greatly favoured at first. It scratched too much, and still lacked the required flexibility. Many writers using it for the first time complained about its performance. But the years passed and as techniques improved, so did the quality of the pen. It is interesting to read that 'When the British Association met in Birmingham [in 1839] steel pens were almost unknown; but when the second visit was made in 1849 the steel pen had risen to a very important place among the manufactures [of Birmingham].' Joseph Gillott, founder of a firm whose name long

Gillott was one of the earliest and best-known steel pen manufacturers. The firm is still in existence though now more concerned with other manufactures. Some steel pen nibs were made until quite recently.

BY COMMAND.

STEEL PEN TO THE — PRECEPT DATED

MAKER QUEEN. APRIL 13, 1840.

JOSEPH GILLOTT, PATENT STEEL PEN MANUFACTURER, Victoria Works, Graham street, Birmingham, has been for Twenty Years engaged in the Manufacture of Steel Pens, and during that time has devoted his unceasing attention to the improving and perfecting this useful and necessary article; the result of his persevering efforts, and numerous experiments upon the properties of the metal used, has been the construction of a Pen upon a principle entirely new, combining all the advantages of the elasticity and fineness of the Quill, with the durability of the Metallic Pen, and thus obviating the objections which have existed against the use of Steel Pens.

The Patentee is proud to acknowledge that a discerning public has paid the most gratifying tribute to his humble, though useful, labours, by a demand for his Pens far exceeding his highest expectations.

The number of Pens Manufactured at the Works of JOSEPH GILLOTT,

From Oct. 1838 to Oct. 1839, was 44,654,702. or 3,721,225 doz. and 2-12ths. or 310,102 gross 1 doz. and 2-12ths.	And from Dec. 1840 to Dec. 1841. was 62,126,928. or 5,177,244 doz. or 431,437 gross.

CAUTION.—J. G. regrets to say, certain disreputable Makers have tried to impose upon the Public a spurious article, bearing the mis-spelled name of the Patentee and sole Manufacturer; thus, "GILLOTT," by omitting the L; and in some instances the final T is omitted, thus, "GILLOT," so as to retain the sound; but the public will please to observe, all the Genuine Pens are marked in full "JOSEPH GILLOTT;" and Venders are desired to note that his Cards of Pens are made up in Packets of one dozen each, and have a label outside with a fac-simile of his Signature.

At the request of persons engaged in tuition, J. G. has introduced his WARRANTED SCHOOL PENS, which are specially adapted to their use, being of different degrees of flexibility, and with fine, medium, and broad points, suitable for the various kinds of writing taught in Schools.

Sold Retail by all Stationers, Booksellers, and other respectable dealers in Steel Pens. Merchants and Wholesale Dealers can be supplied at the Works, Graham street, Birmingham.

remained almost synonymous with pen nibs, was credited with being one of the first to improve the flexibility by making three slits in a nib instead of one – one in the centre of the point and one on each side of the 'shoulder'. After Gillott, the next important name was that of James Perry, who by his promotion of the Perryian system of education almost forced the steel pen on a reluctant public.

In spite of setbacks caused by wars such as the Civil War in America which retarded exports to that continent, and high tariffs as in France, the manufacture of steel pens in Birmingham expanded to become one of its most important industries. It was aided by the introduction of the penny post in 1840 which greatly increased the volume of letter writing among all classes of the population, and also by the gradual increase in education culminating in universal primary education in 1870. Needless to say, the two firms mentioned above were not the only ones to benefit from these social developments and although the trade remained for the most part in Birmingham, the number of firms involved proliferated. It is only in comparatively recent times that the use of the pen has been severely reduced by means of mechanical writing, such as the typewriter, or by the introduction of the ball-point pen and even by the telephone. By 1969 only one firm, British Pens Ltd, formed by the gradual amalgamation of other pen making firms, still survived to carry on the trade which had started in Birmingham 150 years earlier.

The word 'pens' has been repeatedly used in this chapter but of course it should correctly have been written as 'pen nibs', because it was in this part that the invention truly lay. But it was not long before the manufacturers' advertisements were using the word 'pen' in its modern sense. The 'penholder'

PATENT PERRYIAN PENS.—Prices rendered accessible to all Writers. JAMES PERRY & Co., Manufacturers to Her Majesty and H.R.H. Prince Albert, have just introduced a new variety of their excellent Metallic Pens, in boxes containing one gross, &c., in cases containing a quarter of a hundred, and on cards; all of which are manufactured under the protection of their Patents; suitable for every description of writing, and superior to all the ordinary Steel Pens in general use. J. P. & Co. strongly recommend Bankers, Merchants, Exporters of Metallic Pens, and all large buyers to make trial of these articles, in the full confidence they will be found to possess more of the necessary elasticity for the production of good writing than any other Pens at a similar price.

PENS IN BOXES, AND ON CARDS.

DOUBLE PATENT LARGE BARREL PENS, in Boxes, containing one dozen with Holder, or in Boxes of three dozen each, Fine or Medium Points; and on Cards containing nine Pens, with Holder.

DOUBLE PATENT SMALL BARREL PENS, in Boxes, containing one dozen with Holder, or in Boxes of three dozen, six dozen, or twelve dozen each. Fine or Medium Points; and on Cards, containing nine Pens, with Holder.

DOUBLE PATENT PENS, No. 2, in Boxes, containing three dozen, six dozen, or twelve dozen each, with Fine, Medium, or Extra Fine Points.

CURVE-CUT PENS, in Boxes, containing three dozen, six dozen, or twelve dozen each, with Fine or Medium Points; and on Cards, containing nine Pens, with Holder.

PENS IN CASES CONTAINING A QUARTER HUNDRED, WITH HOLDER.

Double Patent Pens, No. 2, with Fine or Medium Points.
Raven Black Pens....No. 2,   „   „
Bronze Pens............No. 2,   „   „

All the other sorts of the Perryian Pens, manufactured by JAMES PERRY & Co., are Sold on Cards as usual.

Sold by all Stationers and Dealers in Metallic Pens, and at the Manufactory, 37 Red Lion square, London.

An advertisement for Perry's pens. From the 'Illustrated Polytechnic Review', vol I (1843)

Just a few from the great variety of penholders available in the second half of the nineteenth century, especially at the cheaper end of the market. This selection was advertised in about 1880. One of the penholders doubles as a monthly calendar.

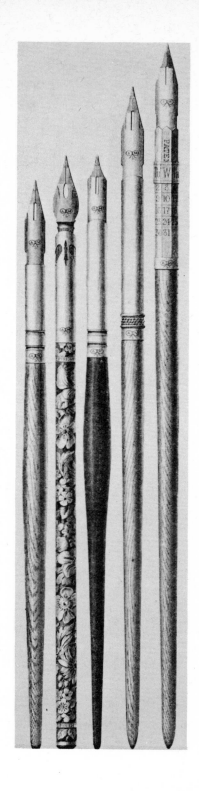

46

required much less ingenuity in its manufacture than did the steel nib. Almost any kind of material could be used as a penholder, and, as the Victorian period progressed, there were few shapes or materials which were not tried out at one time or another, especially in the novelty trade. The commonest form of penholder was wood and this was the cheap kind normally provided for school use. But ivory, silver, ebony, gold, and even glass, were used at times for special pens. For these more expensive ones the metal tip of the nib also received special treatment, being tipped with gold or later with irridium, to give longer life and better flexibility. The trade catalogues of the nineteenth century provided a whole range of styles to choose from to suit all purses – though some of the results can have done little to aid fluent writing. As might be expected of an age which indulged in souvenirs, pens were not excluded. They came marked with 'a present from . . .', or bearing the name of an enterprising advertiser. It is in this field that the modern collector of writing implements on a modest scale can hope to obtain the greatest variety of objects for the minimum outlay. Early examples are difficult to find. Although they were manufactured in great quantities, the nineteenth-century steel pens were not eternal. Many were used till they were worn out, others may have survived and can be found lying in a rusted condition in dark corners of drawers or school cupboards. They were never objects of value, but rather considered disposable as better examples came along. They are not impossible to acquire by the collector who knows what he is looking for. Even the sample given away by a long defunct firm, has a certain charm. Its period lettering may help to date it. Perhaps more interesting are the novelty pens which turn up from time to time (though in decreasing quantities) in junk shops and 'penny trays'. If one is fortunate enough to possess a trade catalogue of the period it is possible to identify and date the various types of nib or penholder. The great variety of the Victorian pen manufacturers' productions is astonishing in these days of ever-increasing uniformity.

If you are fortunate enough to acquire an **early** penholder complete with its original nib, it may be possible to read the name of the manufacturer **on** the nib. Probably the name of the type of nib **will** also be clearly visible – for such items were given names to distinguish them one from another. Some of us can still remember the verse on the old-fashioned enamel advertisement hoardings, frequently found on railway platforms: 'They come **as** a boon and a blessing to men, The Pickwick, **the** Owl and the Waverley pen'. An advertisement of 1870 in *The Reliquary*, vol XI, shows that these names were already well known to users at that date:

MESSRS. MACNIVEN & CAMERON'S PENS.

The newest invention in steel pens which has come under our notice, is the 'Phaeton Pen', just produced by the renowned firm of Macniven and Cameron, of Glasgow. This pen, which is a happy combination of the turned-up and turned-down points, appears to us to be the most skilful and ingenious of any of the various inventions of these marvellously clever makers. We have tried their 'Pickwick Pens' and have been much pleased with them; their 'Owl Pens' and have been delighted; their 'Waverley Pens' and have been charmed; but of all pens the 'Phaeton' have given us the most pleasure, and are the best we have ever written with, for freedom of flow and for ease in use. They are well named, for they literally fly over the paper, and are therefore admirably adapted for rapid writing. Of course it is impossible to say which of the various pens we have named are the best, because some will suit one person best, and others another. All we can say is, that they are all alike good, but that for our own use – for we are rapid and constant writers – the 'Phaeton' is decidedly the best pen we have used.

Reading advertisements for the pen makers' wares tell us a great deal about the industry. They are to be found mainly in old journals or directories for the Birmingham area. But they may also quite often be found in one of the many nineteenth-century periodicals dealing with general subjects such as the *Illustrated*

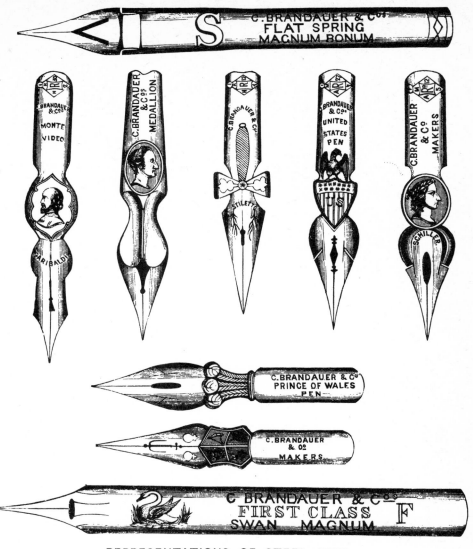

REPRESENTATIONS OF STEEL PENS,

AS MADE BY

C. BRANDAUER & CO.

Manufacturers of Steel Pens of every description,

NEW JOHN STREET PEN WORKS,

BIRMINGHAM.

M. MYERS & SON,

Patentees

FOR

ENGLAND

AND

FRANCE,

RESPECTFULLY CALL THE ATTENTION OF THE PUBLIC
TO THEIR

Patented Galvanized and Arissary

STEEL PENS,

ALSO THEIR

METALLIC POINTS FOR QUILL PENS,

Pens & Holders in all their variety,

FOR HOME TRADE AND EXPORTATION,

CHARLOTTE STREET PEN WORKS,
BIRMINGHAM.

By Her Majesty's · Royal Letters Patent.

JOHN MITCHELL'S

SELF-ADAPTING

METALLIC PENS & PEN HOLDERS

The peculiar advantage of J. MITCHELL'S PATENT PEN is the elasticity of the upper part, which is so constructed that it adapts itself to the Pen Holder, even if much smaller than the Pen, without damaging the nib, thus obviating any inconvenience that has always been experienced by parties using STEEL PENS, and which has entirely prevented many persons from using them.

The PATENT PEN HOLDER possesses a similar advantage as by expansion it accommodates various sized Pens of the ordinary make.

J. M. begs leave respectfully to inform the Merchants, Bankers, and the Public in general, that he continues to manufacture every other description of Steel Pens, for which he solicits their patronage and support.

MANUFACTORY—
48, NEWHALL ST., BIRMINGHAM.

Two advertisements from 'The Directory to the Manufactories' which was published as an appendix to 'Cornish's Stranger's Guide Through Birmingham' (1885)

London News. The advertisement sections of nineteenth-century periodicals make fascinating reading at all times, but for the enquiring collector of writing implements and accessories a special treasure trove can be found: advertisements for inks, pens, pencils, patent inkstands – all help to inform. Other sources of similar information are to be found in reports or catalogues of the big international exhibitions of the nineteenth century starting with the first Great Exhibition at the Crystal Palace, London in 1851. Occasionally a lucky collector will come across not just one nib or pen, but a whole box of them. In this case he will have the pleasure of seeing the original coloured container or wrapping, possibly with embossed lettering, a picture of the factory, the signature of the maker, or other additional gem to enhance the value of his possession.

Unlike the quill where every user was, potentially at least, his own maker, the steel pen from the start needed some help from the machine age. Inevitably as with all new inventions, the pen based itself on an existing pattern. When printing was invented, the first books tried to look like handwritten manuscripts; motor cars were based on the carriage just as the first trains had looked like the contemporary coach. The steel pen first followed the pattern of the existing quill and the metal had to be brought together to form the shape which was natural to the goose feather. But this was a laborious process and one which meant that the resulting product would be costly. The industrial processes in Birmingham during the middle years of the nineteenth century were not static, and methods devised for one piece of equipment were quickly adapted to another. The steel pen benefited from this when Joseph Gillott realised that the nib could be produced from a flat piece of metal, which, given the right sort of machinery, could be cut out in blanks, stamped, and bent. By these processes an improved version of the laboriously hand-produced nibs were mechanically produced by the thousand. And with this mass production costs went down. This not only gave rise to increased sales, but the fact that the average pen could be purchased so cheaply meant that the user was more willing to throw away a worn out one and buy a new pen. It must be remembered too that

The word 'ball-point' is not of recent use, though the technique of the modern pen has little in common with the more traditional steel nib advertised here.

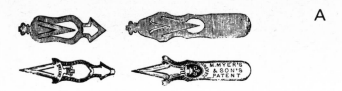

A

B

SLIDE UP—very flexible.　　SLIDE IN THE MIDDLE—medium flexibility.　　SLIDE DOWN—hard.

(a) Patent axissary pens: 'the points of the pens are formed in the body and twisted over by which means an axis is formed on each side of the pen, upon which the point works, and a new and an agreeable elasticity is produced'. (b) A. Sommerville & Co's patent regulating spring slide pens: 'by moving the spring slide up or down the pen, every degree of flexibility is obtained'. Both these exhibits show the amount of experimentation common during this period in attempts to improve the flexibility of the steel pen nib. From 'The Illustrated Catalogue of the Industrial Department, British Division' of the International Exhibition of 1862.

at this time the ink tended to corrode the steel pen, so that it had an inborn obsolescence which worked to the manufacturers' advantage, so long as the cost of the individual item was not too great. In spite of the manufacturing processes applied to the new steel pen and indeed all 'dip' pens up to the present date, they still remain the recognisable brother of the quill. The basic shape has not changed, only the natural curve of the feather has been eliminated. The fountain pen's shape, and the ball-point pen's nib alone have moved away from the traditional style that writers of the past would recognise.

In a work called *British Manufacturing Industries*, which was published in 1876, there appeared an article on the steel pen by George Lindsey of Birmingham. In addition to a history of the manufacture of this important item, he also gave a detailed account of the various processes current at that date. Here is his account of the first processes of manufacture after the steel sheet has been rolled out to the required thinness:

The first process of manufacture now begins, and before the series of operations have been gone through, some fifteen or sixteen distinct processes have to be completed. The strip is carried to the cutting-out room, where the pen first assumes form and shape. Here a number of women and girls are seated at benches, cutting out, by the aid of fly-presses, the future pen from the ribbon of steel before them. This is done with great rapidity, the average product of an expert hand being 200 gross, or 28,800 pens per day. Two pens are cut out of the width of the steel, the broad part to form the tube, if it is to be a barrel pen and the points so cutting into each other, as to leave the least possible amount of waste.

The 'blanks' are next taken to be pierced. The flat blanks are placed separately on a steel die, and, by a half circular action of a lever turning an upright screw, a fine tool is pressed upon the steel, and forms the delicate centre perforation and the side slits which give flexibility to the pen. All this time the metal is in its natural state of elasticity. It is necessary, however, that it should be rendered softer, and for this purpose the pens are again placed in the muffle to be further annealed.

Then comes the marking. On each side and down the middle of the room, a number of young women are seated at work, each of whom, while using her hands to properly adjust the pen and hold it in its place, moves by the action of the foot

Boxes containing pen nibs in the late nineteenth or early twentieth century were sold in decorative wrappers printed in various colours. Victoria & Albert Museum, London (L. 183-1970)

a lever actuated by treadle and wheel, and this marks the pen. When it leaves the hand of the operator, the back of the pen is stamped with the name of a retail dealer at home or abroad, a national emblem, an heraldic device, or the representation of some notability, foreign or domestic, according to the fashion of the day. The rapidity of this process is nearly equal to that of cutting out the blanks, each workwoman marking many thousands of pens in a day.

Up to this time the pen is flat. It has next to be 'raised' into the half-cylindrical form in which we see the finished pen. The flat pen is placed in a groove, and a convex tool made to descend upon it, forcing it into the groove, by means of which it is bent into the required shape.

As a rule, the value of the pen depends very much upon the perfection of the slit.

Among the subsequent important processes was the grinding and slitting of the nib:

The nib is ground by picking up each pen with a pair of pliers, and applying it with a single touch to a rapidly-revolving wheel coated with emery, first lengthwise and then across the nib. This does for the pen the same service that the scraping of a quill with the penknife would do in the case of a quill pen, i.e. weakening certain parts to ensure uniform elasticity.

Next comes the slitting, which is done with the press. In these presses the descending screw has an exactly corresponding chisel cutter, which passes down with precise accuracy, by which movement the slit is made and the pen is completed.

Within the same factory it was common to find other stages of the steel pen business being carried on, such as the manufacture of boxes for the nibs, and the production of penholders, or 'pen-sticks' as they were called. The metal ends into which the pen nibs were fitted were put on by hand. The processes, many of which were carried out by female labour, were much the same in 1890, when Henry Bore wrote *The Story of the Invention of Steel Pens, with a Description of the Manufacturing Processes by Which They Are Produced*. His account was accompanied by pic-

54

SOME PROCESSES IN PEN MAKING.

CUTTING.

STEEL.   SCRAP.

MARKING.   PIERCING.   EMBOSSING.   RAISING.   GRINDING.   SLITTING.

tures 'engraved from pen-and-ink sketches executed by Walter Langley with a Perry's no. 25 pen'.

Henry Bore had made a study of many sources of reference to the steel pen which he quoted, starting with the Bible and passing via Pepys and others to those of more recent date. But he was forced to admit that such references rarely applied to the steel pen with which he was primarily concerned and with which we are still familiar. But for out-of-the-way erudition on the subject his 'genealogy' is worth reading

Beyond improvements in mechanical methods there was little further change in the steel pen until its almost complete disappearance before the universal use of the ball-point pen. It remains in use for more specialised work. Calligraphers, artists, and others who need just the qualities which the steel nib can give, still form a large enough consumer force to justify its continued, though limited, production. In addition to the traditional quill pen, the steel pen is still the best instrument for mapwork and certain calligraphic and design work. Under the name of 'William Mitchell pens' these are still marketed in Britain. William Mitchell founded a steel pen manufactory in the early years of the nineteenth century and the name is perpetuated by British Pens Ltd. It will be noticed that many of the steel pens sold today incorporate a form of reservoir, thus solving one of the problems attendant on the dip pen. Among the modern steel nibs offered by William Mitchell is an italic nib. Modern italic handwriting, whose early advocate was Alfred Fairbank, has been further encouraged by the formation since World War II of the Society for Italic Handwriting. Although italic writers can now be supplied with suitable fountain pens, they are frequently among those who keep up a demand for the more flexible steel pen. The first of such special italic nibs made in 1930 at the instigation of Alfred Fairbank was called 'Flight commander'. Today, the italic writer can have the further choice: a left- or a right-handed nib.

The steel pen, though commercially weak, is not

CUTTING BLANKS

PIERCING.

RAISING OR SHAPING.

SLITTING ROOM.

STAMPING.

The stages in the mass production of steel pen nibs in Birmingham. From 'The Story of the Invention of Steel Pens, with a Description of the Manufacturing Processes by which They Are Produced'.

William Mitchell's advertisement. From 'Robson's London Directory' for 1838.

yet defeated. It retains its importance in the export field, especially where developing countries are concerned. Nowadays, 90 per cent of the production of British Pens Ltd goes abroad, for there are many countries where the traditional steel pen is still the cheapest writing implement. And as long as there are still some writers who prefer beauty to utility it will hold its advantage over the ball-point pen.

58

ROUND HAND PENS

 SQUARE  OBLIQUE

In three patterns  LEFT OBLIQUE

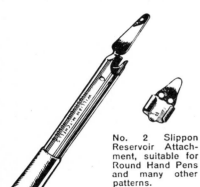

Each pattern is available in 13 Degrees of Point:

No. 00 (3.5 mm.)	**No. 3** (1.4 mm.)
No. 0 (3.3 mm.)	**No. 3½** (1 mm.)
No. 1 (3 mm.)	**No. 4** (0.9 mm.)
No. 1½ (2.5 mm.)	**No. 4½** (0.8 mm.)
No. 2 (2.3 mm.)	**No. 5** (0.75 mm.)
No. 2½ (1.8 mm.)	**No. 5½** (0.7 mm.)
	No. 6 (0.6 mm.)

No. 2 Slippon Reservoir Attachment, suitable for Round Hand Pens and many other patterns.

NO. 548 RESERVOIR PENHOLDER   The ideal Holder for Round Hand Pens

SCROLL Pens

FOR DECORATIVE WRITING AND RULING

In 9 Degrees

No. 10	No. 40	No. 70
No. 20	No. 50	No. 80
No. 30	No. 60	No. 90

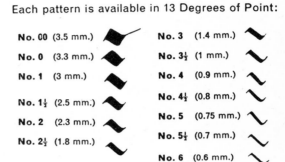

A current advertisement for steel pen nibs and penholders.

4 The Reservoir and Fountain Pen

Quill pen or steel pen, there could be no doubt that one of the great disadvantages of either was the need to constantly replenish the nib with a fresh supply of ink. This inevitably broke the flow of writing which the writing masters recommended to their pupils as being a desirable acquirement. Equally inconvenient was the break in thought which might occur as the pen made its way from paper to inkpot and back again. There was therefore a most urgent need for a pen with a type of reservoir which would obviate to some extent the constant interruptions. 'Reservoir pen' is a reasonable term to use, but why 'fountain pen', since the one thing to avoid was any attempt on the part of the pen to spout ink? The reason for this term has not been traced but its use is surprisingly old. The *New English Dictionary* gives a date of about 1710, quoting the form 'Fountain-inkhorns or fountain pens'. Nevertheless, it must not be presumed that the familiar word was used of the modern fountain pen. Several centuries were to pass before the type was finally (dare one use that word?) perfected.

Early on it was appreciated that for the best results ink must somehow be contained in the barrel of the penholder, from which it could be conveyed in an even flow to the point of writing. The long unsolved problem was how this could be efficiently brought about. When a filled pen is held downwards, the ink it contains can be affected by a variety of forces: gravity, inertia, capillary attraction, air pressure, friction, and the viscosity of the ink itself. The usefulness of the fountain pen would obviously be enhanced if it could be made small enough for the pocket, while containing as large an ink supply as was practical. Such were the needs, and many were the minds occupied in trying to satisfy them.

One of the first attempts to make some form of reservoir was to fix a pocket or recess at the back of the nib. This did at least hold a small amount of ink, perhaps allowing the writer to make one pen dip instead of three for ordinary pens. This was not only difficult to fix to the traditional quill, but also did not necessarily lead to an even supply of the ink held in the reservoir. Such pockets or similar recesses were more easily fixed on the steel nib, and indeed, reservoir steel pen nibs were eventually specially manufactured for this purpose. The real breakthrough came with the 'fountain pen' as we understand it today. The first account of its beginning is found described and illustrated in *The Construction and principal uses of mathematical instruments. Translated from the French of M. Bion ... To which are added ... Those invented or improved by the English.* By Edmund Stone. The work, published in London in 1723, says:

This Inftrument is compofed of different Pieces of Brafs, Silver, &c. and when the Pieces F G H are put together, they are about five Inches long, and its Diameter is about three Lines. The middle Piece F carries the Pen, which ought to be well flit, and cut, and fcrewed into the Infide of a little Pipe, which is foldered to another Pipe of the fame Bignefs, as the Lid G; in which Lid is foldered a Male Screw, for fcrewing on the Cover: as likewife for ftopping a little Hole at the Place 1, and fo hindering the Ink from running through it. At the other End of the Piece F, there is a little Pipe, on the Outfide of which the Top-Cover H may be fcrewed on. In this Top-Cover there goes a Porte-Craion, that is to fcrew into the laft mentioned little Pipe, and fo ftop the End of the Pipe at which the Ink is poured in, by means of a Funnel.
When the aforementioned Pen is to be ufed, the Cover G muft be taken off, and the Pen a little fhaken, in order to make the Ink run freely. *Note*, If the Porte-Craion does not ftop the Mouth of the Piece F, the Air, by its Prefiure, will caufe the Ink all to run out at once. *Note* alfo, that fome of thefe Pens have Seals foldered at their Ends.

An early form of fountain pen. From Edmund Stone's translation of 'The Construction and Principal Uses of Mathematical Instruments' by M. Bion (1723)

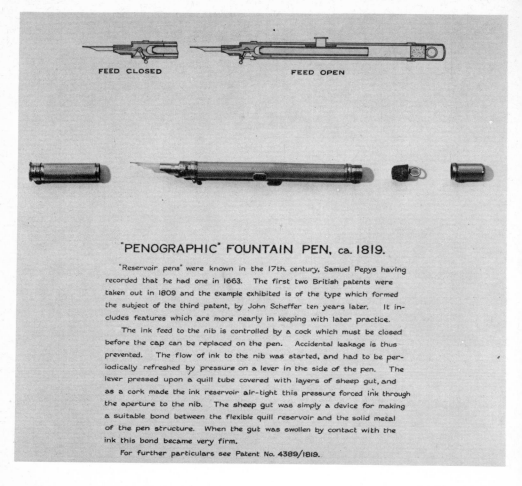

FEED CLOSED   FEED OPEN

"PENOGRAPHIC" FOUNTAIN PEN, ca. 1819.

"Reservoir pens" were known in the 17th. century, Samuel Pepys having recorded that he had one in 1663.   The first two British patents were taken out in 1809 and the example exhibited is of the type which formed the subject of the third patent, by John Scheffer ten years later.   It includes features which are more nearly in keeping with later practice.

The ink feed to the nib is controlled by a cock which must be closed before the cap can be replaced on the pen.   Accidental leakage is thus prevented.   The flow of ink to the nib was started, and had to be periodically refreshed by pressure on a lever in the side of the pen.   The lever pressed upon a quill tube covered with layers of sheep gut, and as a cork made the ink reservoir air-tight this pressure forced ink through the aperture to the nib.   The sheep gut was simply a device for making a suitable bond between the flexible quill reservoir and the solid metal of the pen structure.   When the gut was swollen by contact with the ink this bond became very firm.

For further particulars see Patent No. 4389/1819.

The 'Penographic' fountain pen display as shown in the Science Museum, London. Scheffer widely advertised his pen (see page 63) but many potential users remained dubious as to its efficiency.

An interesting point about Bion's description and portrayal of his fountain pen is that an almost identical one is described and illustrated in *The Dictionary of Arts and Sciences*, published by Owen in 1754–5. The passage has been copied almost word for word and the illustration could have been printed from the same plate, since even the letters used for the explanation are the same. Presumably there can have been remarkably little development in this style of pen if the same description could have been accepted and used in a book published a quarter of a century later.

It must have been this type of rather primitive pen with which Fanny Burney and other eighteenth-century writers who mention 'fountain pens' had to content themselves, since real improvements in the method of construction and design only began to produce their effects in the second half of the nineteenth century. There were so many snags to be overcome that even if one part functioned adequately, another failed to do so. A correspondent who was familiar with the advertisement for 'Scheffer's patent penograph, or writing instrument' wrote to *The Technical Repository* in 1824, enquiring hopefully: 'Does it answer all the purposes for which it is intended? Does not the small hole, through which the ink passes in supplying the pen, quickly become stuffed up by the ink? What is the expense? I have understood that the cost (I know not how correctly) is about 15/–.' Obviously the correspondent had some experience of fountain pens when he wrote his letter and it also indicates the still unsolved problems. Scheffer's penograph was made to be fitted

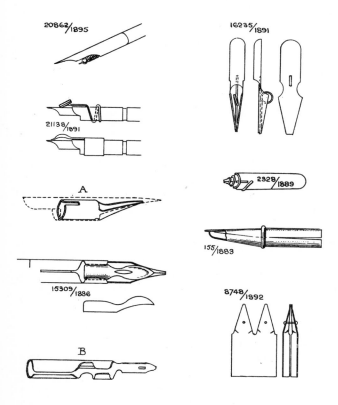

Examples of reservoir pen nibs from the end of the nineteenth century showing patent numbers and dates. From J. P. Maginnis's 'Reservoir, Fountain and Stylographic Pens' in the Journal of the Royal Society of Arts, vol LIII (1905)

with either metallic or quill nibs, but by 1824 the end of the quill nib for general use was already in sight. With the advent of the steel nib and improvement of manufacturing processes, the way was opened for a long series of attempts to solve all the problems attendant upon the production of the perfect fountain pen.

In the meantime the reservoir pen still had a future. It was an improvement on the constant dipping required by the ordinary pen. It was also the subject of many ingenious attempts to perfect its application. Obviously with all the varieties of steel nibs manufactured during the later part of the nineteenth century, a considerable number of different forms of reservoir action were applied to them. Some of the patented forms are illustrated here. The main advantage of the reservoir pen was that it enabled the selected nib to be used without the constant necessity of replenishing the ink. The reservoir pen still has its place today and continues to be manufactured by British Pens Ltd.

It was in 1832 that John Joseph Parker obtained a patent 'for certain improvements in fountain pens', in which he made the first mention of a self-filling

An ingenious – if scarcely practical – suggestion for providing an ink supply. From 'Reservoir, Fountain and Stylographic Pens'.

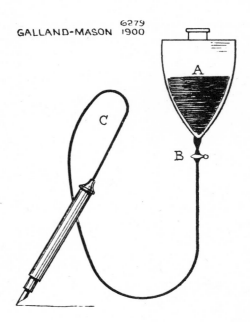

GALLAND-MASON 6279 1900

64

pen. From then on a great variety of patents are recorded all trying to solve the various technical problems involved in producing a really satisfactory pen. Many ingenious ways were devised of getting the ink into the barrel: by means of plungers, pistons, rubber tubes to be operated by hand or by some mechanical device – even by having an ink vessel attached. Having got the ink to the barrel, the problem arose of getting it out for use. The 'feed' part of the fountain pen is the most important part and its perfection was greatly sought after. In an article published by J. P. Maginnis in 1905, an incredible number of different methods are described and many of the resulting instruments are illustrated. Maginnis goes into a great deal of detail about the various patents (some of which are illustrated here), and readers who are interested in the step-by-step technical points in the evolution of the fountain pen are referred to this article. By the end of the nineteenth century some of the best-known makes of fountain pen were in existence, their names being almost household words – eg 'Swan' and 'Waterman' (see fig on page 66). The self-filling fountain pen with its cap had become much as we know it today. Indeed, as Maginnis commented, it was even possible in 1905 to buy a fountain pen (of a sort!) for as little as 3d – or even 1d – 'truly, no-one need be without a fountain pen'.

The fountain pen, like the typewriter, will probably appeal more to the collector who is interested in how things work and the methods by which they reached a particular stage of development. Certainly we have so far considered the fountain pen from the technical point-of-view. But of course the 'works' of the pen were contained in a case which could be either simple or decorative as can be seen from contemporary advertisements. There were slim pens for ladies' handbags, cheap pens for school children, elaborate pens with gold nibs, and elegant boxes or containers for special presentations. But though the detail of their functioning and the decoration of their cases may vary, the shape of the fountain pen, once it had settled down, remained unchanged. Perhaps

PARKER· 6288
1832.

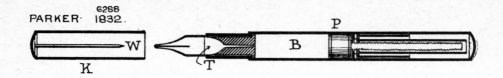

K   W   T   B   P

EDWARDS 7535
1838

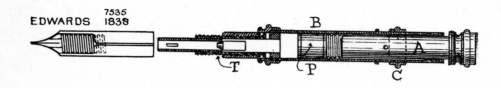

T   P   B   C   A

PRINCE 410
1855.

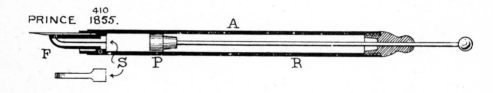

F   S   P   A   R

MOSELEY 2678
1859.

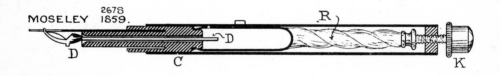

D   C   D   R   K

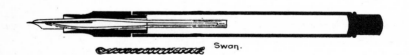

Swan.

B   The Waterman

66

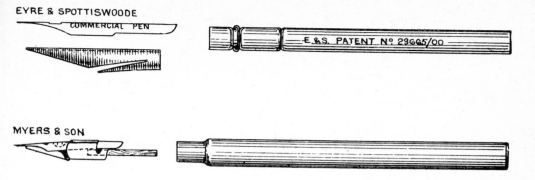

EYRE & SPOTTISWOODE
COMMERCIAL PEN

E.&S. PATENT No 29665/00

MYERS & SON

the only important developments to occur in recent times have been the interchangeable nib and the cartridge method of replacing the ink supply. In the latter the ink supply is completely enclosed in a cartridge which is inserted into the 'stem' of the pen. This system of filling is perhaps the most revolutionary development of the modern fountain pen and has certainly obviated the need for the ink bottle. The interchangeable nib is intended to give the fountain pen as much diversity of use as the dip pen, with its great variety of easily changed nibs. But it is not always successful. It needs to be done with care since the fountain pen has never quite lost the tendency to leak its contents – although almost all pen manufacturers when putting a new model on the market claim it as the final leak-proof fountain pen.

There is no sign that the day of the fountain pen is over. There are still a number of firms in the business and they have adapted their pens to modern needs. One of the interesting developments has been the provision of special 'italic' nibs, to cater for the revival of interest in calligraphy. Another has been the provision of a pen specially geared to the left-handed writer. The acknowledgement of the existence of such a person, let alone the provision of a pen for his use, must have come as a great relief to many children. It is not so long since all children were forced to write with their right hand, regardless of inclination or ability. It will be interesting to see what happens to the fountain pen in the next

The two cheapest fountain pens available in 1905: the top one cost 3d, and the lower one only 1d! From 'Reservoir, Fountain and Stylographic Pens'.

OPPOSITE
Stages in the development of the fountain pen between 1832 and the beginning of the twentieth century. From 'Reservoir, Fountain and Stylographic Pens'.

67

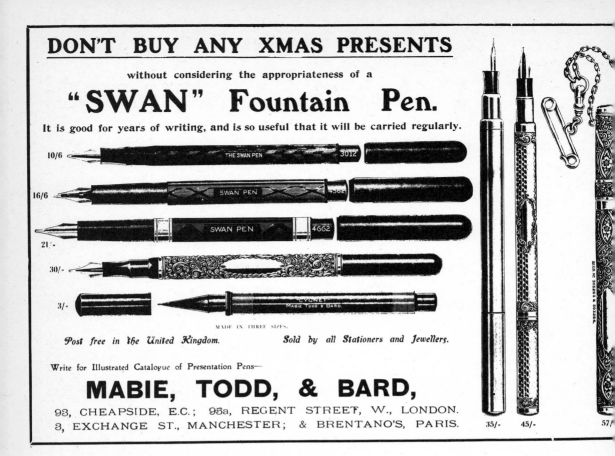

DON'T BUY ANY XMAS PRESENTS

without considering the appropriateness of a

"SWAN" Fountain Pen.

It is good for years of writing, and is so useful that it will be carried regularly.

10/6   THE SWAN PEN   3012

16/6   SWAN PEN   4561

21/-   SWAN PEN   4662

30/-

3/-   CYGNET MABIE TODD & BARD.

MADE IN THREE SIZES.

Post free in the United Kingdom.   *Sold by all Stationers and Jewellers.*

Write for Illustrated Catalogue of Presentation Pens—

MABIE, TODD, & BARD,

93, CHEAPSIDE, E.C.; 95a, REGENT STREET, W., LONDON.
3, EXCHANGE ST., MANCHESTER; & BRENTANO'S, PARIS.

35/-   45/-   57/

Fountain pen cases varied enormously as can be seen from this advertisement which appeared in the 'Illustrated London News' (1903)

decade or two – will it become an instrument of the specialist in the way the steel pen has done? Or will the few remaining faults of the ball-point still ensure that some perfectionists will continue to use the traditional form of pen, for at least some of their writing?

OPPOSITE

A current 'Platignum' advertisement, showing the great variety of fountain pen nibs available for the interchange unit.

Standard nib units

ITALIC SERIES

Fine

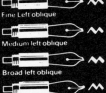

Medium

Broad

Fine Left oblique

Medium left oblique

Broad left oblique

Acute left oblique fine

A Acute left oblique medium

STANDARD SERIES

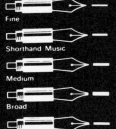

Fine

Shorthand Music

Medium

Broad

Oblique

MR SERIES

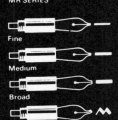

Fine

Medium

Broad

Acute left oblique medium

Acute left oblique broad

LETTERING SERIES

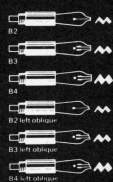

B2

B3

B4

B2 left oblique

B3 left oblique

B4 left oblique

Lettering nib units

Varsity nib units

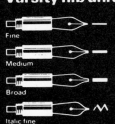

Fine

Medium

Broad

Italic fine

B Italic medium

Fine

Medium

Broad

B2

B3

C B4

Fine left oblique

Medium left oblique

Broad left oblique

B2 left oblique

B3 left oblique

D B4 left oblique

Hooded cartridge nib units

ITALIC SERIES

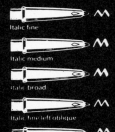

Italic fine

Italic medium

Italic broad

Italic fine left oblique

E Italic med. left oblique

STANDARD SERIES

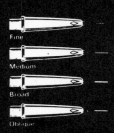

Fine

Medium

Broad

Oblique

Cadet cartridge nib units

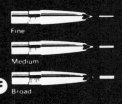

Fine

Medium

F Broad

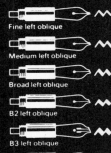

5 Writing Surface and Writing Ink

After using rocks or walls for writing, man turned to other materials. The Romans and the Egyptians made use of papyrus, a reed found growing in Egypt, which, when adequately treated, was suitable for use with the soft point of the reed pen. The Roman schoolboy and the memo writer used waxed tablets as the surface could be erased enabling it to be used again. But it was not with the pith of a reed that the future of writing lay, but rather with the skin of an animal. It was said that the embargo placed by Egypt on the export of papyrus forced her rival in the field of learning at that time to experiment with an alternative form of writing material. For the Library of Pergamon in Asia Minor considered itself as important as the famous Library at Alexandria. Not to be thwarted by a lack of the essential material for books, the Pergamenes developed a new kind of writing surface from the skins of animals. The Greek for this material (vellum or parchment) is περγαμηνή (the German is 'Pergament') which lends some support to the old tale. But whatever the origins of vellum, it was a long time before it entirely supplanted papyrus in the Roman world.

For some time papyrus and vellum existed side by side, as did the two formats of roll and codex. The majority of the classical texts were written in roll form on papyrus. Roman paintings show them lined up in a cupboard with their title tags visible for the benefit of the user. But there is no doubt that the use, for reference purposes, of a text written in scroll form is very limited. To reach the required part of the text the whole length may have to be unrolled. This was unsatisfactory and the codex, was obviously more manageable and gradually superseded all other forms except in the case of some documentary or legal material. The word codex is used to describe a gathering of leaves which resembles the modern book. But at the period when Christianity was but recently recognised as the official religion of the Roman Empire (Constantine the Great proclaimed freedom of worship in 313) the codex was made up not of paper (as today) but of vellum.

Vellum remained in use throughout most of the Middle Ages and for legal and other documents its use continued until recent times. It is still preferred on certain occasions, such as formal addresses to the sovereign, or for charters and other similar documents.

Vellum is made from the skin of sheep or goats, the best material coming from the young of either of those species. It has to be specially treated for writing purposes. Since both sides of the skin are used, it is possible when looking at a piece of vellum to distinguish the outer 'hair' side from the inner 'flesh' side with its smoother surface. In the make-up of a book, it was usually so contrived that hair side met hair side, and smooth side met smooth side. The great advantage of vellum was that it was extremely durable and manuscripts written as early as the fifth century still survive today. Although vellum is a flexible material, it is nevertheless an organic object and has a life of its own – as any one who has tried to unravel an old document will have discovered. The pages of manuscripts dating from the Middle Ages which now exist in libraries and museums often

Some of the stages in the preparation of vellum (or parchment). From Diderot's 'Encyclopédie; ou, dictionnaire raisonné des sciences, des arts et des métiers' (1751–80)

show curl, bubble, or other marks of the skin from which they were made. Yet it was an extremely suitable material for writing on once it had been prepared for use. The main transformation from living animal to writing surface would normally have been done outside the scriptoria of the monasteries, but the final polish given to the skin was very much the work of the individual scribe. Just as today the purchaser of writing paper can choose from a variety of writing surfaces of varying degrees of smoothness, so the medieval writer could choose the surface most suited to his particular style and quill. The final treatment of the surface to free it from grease was done with a fine pumice kept in a pounce pot which became a regular piece of scribal equipment.

It was to some extent its very usefulness that led to vellum being superseded in its turn by paper. It was never cheap – after all the shape of the animal meant that the resulting skin never had a very large area without blemishes or signs of the animal's anatomy. The material was used as economically as

72

possible, the scribe writing in a small hand for every day matters, and even re-using the material wherever possible ('palimpsest' is the word for a manuscript which has been re-used). Following the invention of printing and the production of books by mechanical means, the inconvenience of the vellum sheet became even more apparent and its cost of more concern. A few books continued to be printed on vellum. These were usually special editions for much more care was needed in their production than when printing on paper. Some printing on vellum is still carried out today.

Paper, believed to have been first produced in China, was introduced into Spain by the Moors and then passed into Italy and France. The early medieval paper was made from shredded rags which gave it its tough pliant quality, although this type of paper tended to be very porous. From the late fourteenth century it was sized with animal glue which overcame this defect to some extent. Paper had been imported into England in small quantities but it was not until the late fifteenth century that it became at all common. The rags had first to be sorted and graded, and then shredded. (Even today when paper manufacture is carried out almost entirely by mechanical means, the first two stages still have to be done by hand.) The rags were then made into a pulp with the addition of water (nowadays the size is also added at this stage). This rag pulp was scooped up in a tray, the shape and size of which affected the proportions of the finished sheet of paper, and the water was allowed to drain away. Remaining operations included further draining and pressing before the sheet of paper was ready for the pen and ink. In the beginning the great difficulty was to produce a surface on which the pen could write easily, and on which the ink would remain visible. For many reasons it was some time before paper completely replaced vellum in general use: in non-industrial societies natural material is cheaper than the manufactured one; animals, from whose skins vellum could be made, were all around, but the preparation of paper required special skills and conditions which were not always available. Paper, especially in its early form, could not be used more than once. It was liable to deteriorate in certain conditions and was generally more easily destroyed than vellum. As long as vellum was not needed for the mechanics of printing its disadvantages were less important, but as the manufacture of paper became more common, it was gradually replaced for nearly all purposes.

Starting as a series of hand processes, the manufacture of paper was gradually facilitated by the introduction of various labour-saving devices, some of which can be seen in the eighteenth-century engraving from Diderot's encyclopedia. Here we see a few men working simple methods. But by the time we reach the early nineteenth century we find the beginning of more sophisticated methods and the signs of mass production, as in the illustration from *Galerie industrielle* (1822). The nineteenth century saw the complete mechanisation of paper-making processes and also the substituting, for cheaper papers, of mechanical wood pulp, esparto grass, and similar materials instead of rags. Some hand-made paper is still produced by traditional processes. Early paper

Some stages in the preparation of paper during the eighteenth century. From Diderot's encyclopedia.

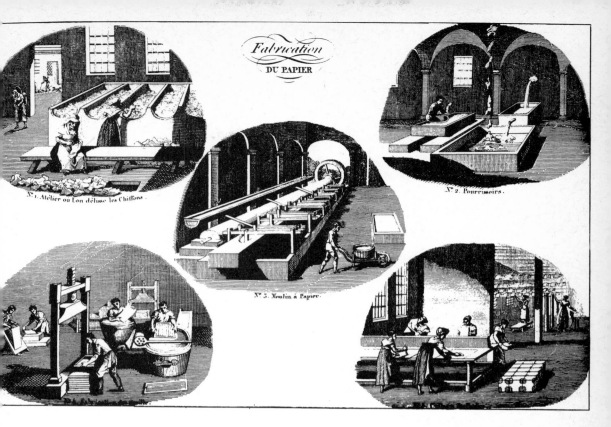

Nº 1. Atelier ou l'on délisse les Chiffons.

Nº 2. Pourrissoirs.

Nº 3. Moulin à Papier.

tended to be yellowish and rather coarse, and the difference in the quality and colour of the paper of old letters from that of modern samples is very noticeable. If it is possible to acquire an old letter, hold the sheets to the light so that you can see the lines in the paper caused by the wire mesh through which the water was originally drained. Sometimes the sheets will include the manufacturer's watermark and, occasionally, the date as well. This will help to identify the period at which a letter or document was written and possibly the type of pen used to write on it.

COLLECTING WRITING PAPER

There is little further to be said on the development of writing paper, for the methods of production changed little over the years, but one aspect at least can provide material for the collector. This is the popularity in the mid-nineteenth century of writing paper with engraved views at the top. It is still occasionally possible to come across unused sheets of

Stages in the manufacture of paper during the nineteenth century. From 'Galerie industrielle; ou, applications des produits de la nature aux arts et métiers' (1822)

Two examples of mid-nine-teenth-century decorative writ-ing paper. Both illustrations are engraved, but the 'Hast-ings' sheet also has an em-bossed ornamentation.

this paper, showing holiday resorts and views, or the previous owner's local town. When the rage for engraved pictorial writing paper passed, it became popular to have a crest or monogram on the note-paper, which was later stamped on the back of the envelope as well. This habit has not entirely passed away. Some commercial firms and hotels still have their situations or business premises pictured at the head of their notepaper. Collecting these charming old engraved sheets, especially ones with pictures of vanished hotels and forgotten commodities, can give social or topographical information as well as pleasure.

Another feature of writing paper which should be mentioned is mourning stationery. Many readers will have seen the black-bordered envelope still occasionally used on the continent. In Victorian England especially, the period of mourning was strictly regulated as were the various items used by the bereaved. Women's journals of the period frequently contained information on the subject – sometimes in answer to readers' enquiries. The details concerned not only the amount of mourning to be worn, for how long, and for what degree of relationship, but even discussed the depth of the black border to be placed on the stationery used during the mourning period. This was allowed to become narrower as the costume of the bereaved lightened in colour. The degree and extent of Queen Victoria's mourning for Prince Albert was followed in times of loss by her faithful subjects. Items of mourning stationery are interesting to collect, though perhaps only one or two samples are wanted in a collection. The ritual of mourning went further than paper and envelope and for the collector of writing equipment there is black sealing wax, black leather blotters, and jet paperknives. All these things in isolation may be puzzling, but seen together and against the social background of the time, they are self-explanatory.

Although mourning stationery, together with the sheets of engraved headings or monograms, are perhaps the most striking examples of 'speciality' writing paper, some collectors may like to search for coloured or gilt-edged examples. All these may be found from time to time, though by their very nature sheets of writing paper are rarely found in perfect, unused condition. This is even more true of earlier, hand-made examples. But occasionally sheets have survived slipped between pages of a book or at the back of a drawer. Perhaps even a letter itself may fall from a volume, placed there by some long-forgotten writer.

INK

Having obtained a suitable pen, and material upon which to write, the scribe's next requirement was ink. A clue to the sort of liquid this might be can be found in the derivation of the word itself. It comes from the Latin *encaustum*, which derived from a Greek word meaning to burn in, and this is to some extent what the early writing fluid did. There were in fact two kinds of medieval ink. One was prepared from a combination of iron salt and oak galls, which tended to become dark brown with age and which literally 'burnt' itself into the writing surface. The other kind of ink was made from a suspension of carbon (such as lampblack) in a mixture of gum and water. This produced a much blacker effect but had certain disadvantages: the writing remained on the surface, and if the gum with which it was mixed became brittle, the writing perished. Moreover, ink made in this fashion required constant stirring to keep the carbon in suspense and so prevent the pen from becoming clogged. When we think of ink today, we tend to visualise an item that can be bought neatly packaged ready for use in bottles. But, just as in the past most people prepared their own quills, so many made their own ink. Recipes for good ink appear in various medieval texts, and when the writing masters began to publish their copybooks in the sixteenth and seventeenth centuries, they frequently included their own special method of preparing a suitable writing fluid. Edward Cocker, a prolific calligrapher and teacher, writing in the last half of the seventeenth century in London, nearly always included a recipe for ink among his other instructions to the pupil. They follow very closely those given in the Palatino book published in 1540, and no doubt reflect a recipe that had been used for many years before that. One can imagine the ritual attendant upon writing when so much preparation had to be done before one word could be written.

Here is Cocker's method of making good ink as given in *The Pen's Triumph*, published in 1658:

To make Ink.

Take three Ounces of Galls which are small and heavy and crisp, put them in a vessell of three pints of Wine, or of Rain-water, which is much better, letting it stand so infusing in the Sun for one or two dayes ; Then take two Ounces of Coppris, or of Roman Vitrial, well colour'd and beaten small, stirring it well with a stick, which being put in, set it again in the Sun for one or two dayes more. Stir all together, adding two Ounces of Gum Arabique of the clearest and most shining, being well beaten. And to make your Ink shine and lustrous, add certain pieces of the Barque of Pomgranat, or a small quantity of double-refin'd Sugar, boyling it a little over a gentle fire. Lastly, pour it out, and keep it in a vessell of Glasse, or of Lead well covered.

One of the very earliest of the medieval sources had, however, offered a very different recipe. In *De diversis artibus*, a twelfth-century account of many contemporary processes, the monk Theophilus offered a method of making ink which was quite as complicated as that of later writers:*

* From the version translated and edited by C. R. Dodwell, in parallel texts of Latin and English (1961).

To make ink, cut for yourself some wood of the hawthorn – in April or May before they produce blossom or leaves – collect them together in small bundles and allow them to lie in the shade for two, three or four weeks until they are fairly well dried out.

Then have some wooden mallets, and with them pound these thorns on a hard piece of wood until you can completely peel off the bark, which you immediately put in a barrel full of water. When you have filled two, three, four or five barrels with bark and water, allow them to stand like this for eight days until the water has drawn off all the sap of the bark. Then put this water into a very clean pot or into a cauldron, place it on the fire and heat it. From time to time, put some of this bark into the pot so that, if there is any sap left in it, it can be boiled out, and, when you have heated it for a little, take it out and put in some more. This done, boil down what remains of the water to a third (of its original quantity), pour it from this pot into a smaller one and continue to heat it until it becomes black and begins to thicken, taking particular care that you do not add any water except that which was mixed with the sap. When you see it become thick, add a third part of pure wine, put it in two or three new pots and continue to heat it until you see that it develops a kind of skin at the top.

However convenient it may have been to have fresh ink readily available and to have it made to the consistency required by each individual, not every writer was prepared to accept such a counsel of perfection. Cheaper forms of ink for the schoolboy, for commercial purposes, and for those unable or unwilling to follow such instructions as have been given above, could be bought during the eighteenth century from a travelling inkseller. A familiar sight in towns, he appears in many of the books of street

Come buy my fine Writing Ink!

**Through many a ſtreet and many a town
The Ink-man ſhapes his way;
The truſty Aſs keeps plodding on,
His maſter to obey.**

cries published during the eighteenth and nineteenth centuries, with his ass or donkey carrying the barrels of ink for sale to passing customers. The itinerant vendor was not the only source of ink, it could also be bought in the shops where writing books were published and at stationers in general. Thomas Rooks, who published the work of Peter Gery, another seventeenth-century writing master, made sure this fact was not overlooked by adding after his own name on the title page 'who sells the best ink'.

Ink suitable for the quill was not at all suited to the steel pen and this was one of the great problems which faced developers of the metal nib. Even with careful wiping after use the steel nib corroded in time, so a new basis for ink was required. The manufacturers of inks were conscious of the shortcomings of their wares, especially as the steel pen increased in popularity during the 1840s and 1850s. The steel pen manufacturers also realised that the quality of the ink could damage the reputation of their pens, and so it was not surprising to find that some of the well-known pen makers also began to produce their own special ink. Henry Stephens set up the first ink factory in 1834 and 'Stephens' ink' became one of the best-known writing fluids. In an advertisement

Henry Stephens set up the first ink factory in 1834. This advertisement is from 'Robson's London Directory for 1838'.

of 1843 the suitability of Stephens' ink for the new steel pens is emphasised, but just as a precaution, the firm also offered its own 'select steel pens':

COMPOSITION FOR WRITING WITH STEEL PENS.
STEPHENS' WRITING FLUID.

THESE COMPOSITIONS, which have so remarkably extended the use of the STEEL PEN, are brought to very great perfection, being more easy to write with, more durable, and in every respect preferable to the ordinary Ink. In warm climates they have become essential. They consist of:—

An INSTANTANEOUS BLACK INK.

A BLUE FLUID, changing to an intense Black colour.

PATENT UNCHANGEABLE BLUE FLUIDS, remaining a deep Blue colour.

A SUPERIOR BLACK INK, of the common character, but more fluid.

A SUPERIOR CARMINE RED for Contrast Writing.

A CARBONACEOUS RECORD INK, unchangeable by any Chemical Agent.

Also, a new kind of MARKING INK for Linen: and Inkholders adapted for preserving Ink from Evaporation and Dust. Bottles at 3d. each, convenient for writing from, are prepared, which will enable those who may wish to try either of these articles to do so at a small expense.

Prepared by HENRY STEPHENS, the Inventor, 54 Stamford street, Blackfriars road, London, and sold by Stationers and Booksellers.

N.B. These unchangeable Blue Fluids are Patent Articles; the Public are therefore cautioned against imitations, which are infringements; to sell or use which is illegal.

STEPHENS' SELECT STEEL PENS.

The utmost possible care having been bestowed upon the manufacture of these articles so as to procure the highest finish, they can be confidently recommended both for flexibility and durability.

In the same issue of *The Polytechnic Review*, the well-known pen makers, J. Perry & Co, advertised their own 'Perryian Limpid Ink' as the most suitable to be used with their pens:

PERRYIAN LIMPID INK.

This Ink has a flowing property peculiar to itself, and does not corrode Metallic Pens as other Inks.—In bottles, 6d., 1s., and 2s. each. Also, in POWDER, 6d. and 1s. per Packet. Sold by all Stationers and Dealers in Metallic Pens, and at the Manufactory, 37 Red Lion square, London.

The discovery of aniline dyes in 1856 made a great difference to the composition of ink and enabled some of the more corrosive properties to be gradually eliminated. Nevertheless the experiments to find a perfect writing fluid continued. A good ink needs many differing qualities in order to be completely acceptable. It must run freely, but not spread; it should not smell, or be liable to go bad; it should dry easily; it should not harm the paper on which it is used, and, of course, it should not harm the writing instrument. Some people in the past would certainly have added that it should be washable – ink stains, ink blots, and similar fatalities, occurred with great frequency in the days before fountain pens and ball-point pens.

Ink was also supplied in powdered form as offered in the Perry's ink advertisement. This was particularly popular with bulk buyers, among them schools – especially after the introduction of compulsory primary education in 1870. If not purchased in powdered form, ink for schools and other large-scale purchasers could be obtained in large stoneware jars, from which the ink was decanted as required. These jars, once a common sight, can still be found occasionally, though rarely with their contents intact. Tins of powdered ink have almost completely disappeared although I found one in a Shropshire village school cupboard not so long ago. This type of ink was however inferior and for more expensive pens a ready-to-use ink was, and still is, sold in glass bottles of varying sizes. With the school ink came the paraphernalia used for its distribution which has now vanished with the rest of the apparatus. It would have been the duty of one pupil, or perhaps the monitor, to issue the daily supply of ink. He would have used a tray-like container with special holes to keep the desk inkpots steady while they were refilled. This tray also had handles so that the monitor could carry the full pots round the class and hand them out. Trays like these have mostly disappeared as have the once-common china inkwells with the maker's name lettered round the rim. Of course examples of such things do exist, and can still be acquired from time to time. But they are breakable objects and so ordinary that few people thought to preserve them. They are among the writing items which have little charm save for their association with generations of childish endeavour.

So far only black ink has been considered since it has at all times been the kind in greatest demand. Second in importance has been red ink. Indeed the use of red ink in early handwritten manuscripts has added words to the language. To *rubricate* a book meant to put in the headings in red, especially the major feast days in the calendar and so we have 'red letter days'. The improvement in ink also led to greater experiments in colour and among the modern permanent inks in general supply are red, green, blue, blue-black and turquoise. In the 1930s a washable ink was developed but its colour range has tended to be limited to blue. Other types of 'ink' are currently in use but they have not derived from the traditional writing fluid. The kind used in the ball-point pen is nearer to printing ink, while that in the felt-tip pen has a spirit base.

Container Problems: Ink, Pounce, Pens etc.

꙳꙳꙳꙳꙳꙳꙳꙳꙳꙳꙳꙳꙳꙳꙳꙳꙳꙳꙳꙳꙳꙳꙳꙳꙳꙳꙳꙳꙳꙳꙳

Pens and ink have been discussed, but not how to store them ready for use. Of all the writing accessories available for the collector perhaps the inkpot or inkstand is the most attractive. It comes in all shapes and sizes and materials, and is therefore available to all pockets. A collection, while making an attractive display, can also be fairly easily stored.

The scribe certainly could not begin his work without ink, but without a container for that ink he was equally helpless. The ink container figures prominently in nearly all the early representations of writers at work, affording the student a very good idea of its shape and development. In all unsophisticated societies natural objects are more easily available than man-made ones, however simple. It is not surprising therefore that some of the earliest ink containers should be made of horn, and in many cases were used more or less in their natural state, ie hornshaped. But a horn, especially one containing ink, does not readily *stand* upon a desk, and so we find special provision for such 'ink horns' shown in the manuscript illustrations. They often appear fixed in a hole on the side or top of a

(a) One of the cheapest ink-pots, common in offices, was made in pewter or white metal, with a porcelain inkwell. (b) An olive wood inkstand, with a metal bird holding a pen. (c) An inkstand of iridescent glass made up of four balls decorated with hand-painted flowers. The hinge and mount are of brass. (d) An enamelled bronze and iron inkstand, with a pen brush. Being so heavy it also served as a paperweight. (e) An inkstand consisting of two compartments of cut crystal glass with brass hinges and mounts. It has three grooved steps for penholders, pencils, etc.

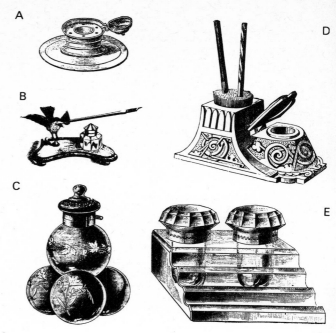

writing desk. It is not surprising either, that when the inkhorn began to be made in other materials, such as wood, pottery, *cuir bouilli* (leather), or metal, its form frequently followed the original pointed horn shape. Sometimes this elongated shape was intended to allow a space for the storage of the pen as well as the ink. But it was appreciated that any suitable object which would hold liquid would also hold ink, and so by imitating other containers the inkpot began quite early to assume the varied shapes which can be found again and again through-out the centuries. An inkpot has to have certain basic characteristics in order to fulfil its function. It should stand or fit easily on the writing desk. It should have a solid bottom or base so that it is not easily knocked over, and it should not be too deep, otherwise the upper part of the pen (or quill) will get inky. It needs a fairly narrow neck to prevent evaporation, and a lid to prevent dust and other impurities from contaminating the ink. Within these general terms all sorts of variations are possible. By

the Middle Ages all the most obvious shapes were already to be found. Next to horn in popularity was that very versatile material, leather. This was always quite plentiful, especially since the medieval economy required the autumn slaughter of animals, and therefore reasonably cheap compared with glass or pottery. It was also tough and hard wearing. In its most commonly-used form for containers, it was known as *cuir bouilli* – literally 'boiled leather'. It was subjected to a process which not only toughened the

Two horn inkwells of the medieval period, bearing incised compass-drawn ornaments. The rim of the left-hand one was pierced with holes so that it could be suspended from a cord. London Museum (A. 242, A. 13339)

An English inkwell in 'cuir bouilli', decorated with stamped figures of saints. About 1¾ in high, it dates from the late fifteenth to the early sixteenth century. London Museum (A. 28570)

material but also allowed the application of decorative motifs to the finished article. Surviving inkhorns frequently show an embossed pattern or design, which can be compared with that found on other domestic items made of the same material. Metal containers were also used since this material again was a long-lasting one. But metal, unlike glass or pottery, was more subject to ink corrosion and so for certain types of inkhorn an inner container of glass, pottery, or horn was essential.

Many scribes needed to carry their writing implements around with them. A monk in a cloister or clerk in an office could arrange his material in a permanent setting. But just as the medieval court itself was peripatetic, so were its servants. Manorial and other officials, merchants or tradesmen and their attendant clerks, all travelled about in the course of their work. The clerk had to be able to settle down and write wherever he was needed. We therefore find that many of the medieval inkhorns have places through which a strap or thong was fitted in order to attach the container to the scribe's belt. In the illustration showing St John writing, his symbol – the eagle – is very obligingly holding his inkpot for him, dangling from its cord or strap. Attached to the other end is the 'penner' or container for pens. Just as the scribe needed ready access to his ink, so he needed his quills and pen knife to hand. These too were carried at his waist, or even slung around his neck as a badge of office, and both would probably be of leather as it was a reasonably light material.

The inkhorns and penners so far considered were mainly for the use of the professional scribe. But literacy increased considerably during the Middle Ages and the dawning of the Renaissance led to such an upsurge of interest in intellectual matters that even the princes found it important to know how to write with fluency. The days when literacy was confined to the clergy had long since passed. Businessmen, traders, travellers, and mere letter writers began to leave behind a written record of their existence. For such writers a new kind of inkpot was required. It was likely to be more permanently in

Two late nineteenth-century papier-mâché inkstands. The more elaborate one on the right is decorated with painted flowers and inlaid mother-of-pearl. It has two ink bottles and a stamp box. The one on the left has a stork pattern on a gold background.

one place than the inkpot belonging to the wandering scribe, and so could be made of heavier material and be more elaborately ornamented. For princely owners, precious metals would have been used, and the elaborations found in other furniture and effects were applied to the inkstand too. The Renaissance, delighting in the strange and recondite, made its containers in all shapes. One bronze inkpot in the Victoria and Albert Museum shows a monkey stealing a child from a cradle, the cradle forming the inkpot. Another, also in bronze, is heavily decorated with the family arms. Such inkpots were meant to stand solidly and decoratively on the owner's writing desk or table.

A variety of inkpots began to appear in portraits as well as in various other appropriate scenes. Religious pictures still showed St Jerome or the Evangelists at work, but pictures or prints of merchants, money-changers, poets and other literary men also frequently included illustrations of inkpots, quills and various other writing equipment. For business work, the pewter inkpot began to replace the leather inkhorn or inkpot. For richer people, composite containers began to appear in which items intended for several different but allied functions were housed together, such as the inkpot and the penholder. A third item often associated with these two, either as a separate item or combined with them to form an inkstand or 'standish,' was the pounce pot.

The pounce pot had a long history and changed its function several times during its existence.

Originally it was used by the medieval scribe for the final smoothing or degreasing of the vellum surface prior to writing. At this stage one of a number of substances might be used, among them powdered pumice, cuttlefish or sanderach (a form of resin). As paper gradually replaced vellum it was not so much a surface scouring that was needed but rather something to prevent the ink sinking into the early type of paper. For this function powdered sanderach could be used, and it was contained in a pot with a perforated lid so that it could be easily shaken over the writing surface. In some pounce pots (also called sand dredgers or sand boxes) the perforated lid was saucer shaped, so that the pounce could be tipped back from the paper for re-use.

But the use of pounce was to change again before modern developments made its employment unnecessary. As writing paper improved, the surface ceased to need pouncing. On the other hand, the ink now no longer sank into the imperfectly-sized material but remained wet and liable to smudge. So the pounce pot was filled with chalk powder or, more commonly, with biotite (powdered magnesium mica), which was used to 'blot' the ink. When reading old letters it is still possible to catch an

An imitation brass inkstand.

91

A bronze Florentine pounce pot in the shape of a frog with a shell, dating from the sixteenth century. Victoria & Albert Museum, London (6904-1860)

occasional sparkle from the ink where a fragment of mica has dried into the writing. But the days of the pounce pot were numbered. 'Blotting' paper is said to have been discovered by a lucky error, through a workman's omission of the vital ingredient of size in the manufacture of some paper. It came into common use in the nineteenth century although examples dating from much earlier do exist. The pounce pot was thus removed from the inkstand, and the blotter or blotting pad took its place on the writing table. Many pounce pots were made 'en suite' with ink-pots but they can also be found as individual objects. They were made of a great variety of materials: leather, wood, pewter, silver and so on.

A 'medieval' mounted inkstand with cut crystal bottles, nickel, silver or gilt engraved mounts. Made in walnut and ebonised wood, it has two pen hollows and a drawer.

Although the inkstand most commonly consisted of a pounce pot, inkpot, and pen tray, there were other variations or additions. A small square box is sometimes found as a component of the inkstand; occasionally, instead of a box, a small drawer. This was the wafer box or drawer. Before the introduction of the envelope and the prepaid penny postage, letters were folded and sealed with wafers, a supply of which was kept handily for the writer with his other equipment. Even when adhesive envelopes came into common use the practice of using wafers continued, though by then, the fixing of a wafer or decorative seal was no longer essential but merely fashionable. The wafer boxes or drawers did not, like the pounce pot, become obsolete since they could be equally serviceable as stamp boxes and, of course, may still be used for this purpose.

Made by Paul de Lamerie, this English silver inkstand has a London hall-mark for 1729–30. On the tray stands an inkpot, a sandbox, and a bell to summon the servant. Victoria & Albert Museum, London (M. 155-c-1939)

Two other adjuncts to the inkstand which may be briefly dealt with, were the taper stand and the handbell. Some of the more elaborate silver inkstands incorporated a small handbell – for summoning the servant to take a letter after it had been written. Occasionally, a taper stand, or even a small candlestick, was associated with an inkstand. This related to the necessity of sealing letters in the days before the use of adhesively-sealed envelopes. A taper stand from which the taper is missing may puzzle the collector as to its correct use. But there are usually indications of a space for the length of a taper to be stored, and for it to be gradually unwound as need arose, which assist identification.

In the days before the invention of the fountain pen, everyone who wrote with any frequency needed to possess an inkpot and many people chose to have an inkstand which combined the ink container with

A multi-purpose writing accessory, in which all the scribal aids are combined in one unit. A typical piece of Victorian ingenuity from 'The Reliquary', vol 20 (1879–80)

MESSRS. DEYKIN & SONS "ROWLAND HILL" INKSTAND.

IT is seldom indeed that we have seen any article of actual utility in which Art and design are so thoroughly and so pleasantly combined with true excellence of manufacture as in the " Rowland Hill " Inkstand, just introduced by Messrs. Deykin & Sons, of the Venetian Works, Birmingham. This excellent article— for no other term would be at all appropriate to it—is assuredly the most elegant, the most useful, and the most perfect in all its parts of any that has of late come before us, and it is therefore with peculiar pleasure that we call our readers special attention to its merits. The " Rowland Hill " is, in fact, not only

an inkstand, but is a combination of desk-formed paper and envelope case, double inkstand, and letter weigher. Massively formed of electro-plate, and delicately chased on its ends and lid, the effect is much heightened by the prettily-formed rails being electro-gilt. These gold railings harmonise excellently well with the silver of the rest of the article, and with the elegant cut-glass inkstands, capped and mounted in the same metal. From the back rises an elegantly carved rack, from which is suspended a Salter's letter balance. Thus the whole thing is complete, and comprises desk-like receptacle for paper and envelopes, bottles for black and for red ink, letter weigher, and pen rack. It is of convenient size, remarkably well made in every part, and of faultless taste both in general outline and in ornamentation. It is eminently suited for the drawing-room or boudoir of the home of taste, and as a wedding present, or a gift for the present or any other season of friendly and loving offerings, is unequalled. Messrs. Deykin and Sons deserve all praise for producing so thoroughly good and artistic an article, and we have no hesitation in giving it hearty commendation.

other scribal necessities. The style of such items reflected the fashion of the day, repeating on a smaller scale the shapes and decorative motifs which can be traced in other objects associated with daily life. But just as the quality of clothes or furniture varied with the financial or social position of the owner, so did the writing implements he used. The poorer people would make use of treen (wood), pewter, plain glass, or simple pottery. The richer would have inkstands of silver, or fine porcelain, with crystal inkpots, some of them even with gold or jewelled fittings. A great many examples of all kinds have survived, especially those which have an intrinsic value. If one cannot hope to collect the grander examples, it is usually fairly easy at least to see them. Museums are the obvious places where some of the finest pieces – perhaps made for a sovereign or other well-known personality – have come to rest. In addition, nearly every country house open to the public displays, in one of its rooms, a desk with its attendant inkstand. Such notable porcelain factories as those of Derby or Worcester produced delicately painted inkstands and in the eighteenth century some were designed by famous silversmiths, like Paul de Lamerie. When

English silver inkstand, late seventeenth century. This inkstand contains space for pens, pounce, wafers, and ink. Victoria & Albert Museum, London (M.599-1924)

Porcelain inkstand. Derby c 1820. In royal blue and gold on white it has a painted landscape decoration in the pen tray. Victoria & Albert Museum, London (C. 1278-c-1919)

the quill pen had been superseded by the steel pen and the pounce pot had disappeared, obviously a change took place in the composition of the inkstand. With the introduction of prepaid penny postage a tremendous increase in letter writing took place. More and more people began to need inkstands, so that in the Victorian period we find a great variety. Other accessories were now added to the conventional items: a stationery rack, letter-scales, perhaps a calendar. One manufacturer even offered a combined ink and cigar stand! And there was the highly recommended 'Rowland Hill' inkstand of about 1880, 'not only an inkstand, but ... a combination of desk-formed paper and envelope case, double ink-stand, and letter weigher' which was 'massively formed of electro-plate ... with elegant cut-glass inkstands'. But just as the Renaissance owner had delighted in fantastic forms of inkstand, so the Victorians in their passion for novelty made ink-pots and inkstands in a variety of different shapes. In addition to the novelty trade there were also imitations of earlier styles, and the eclecticism of the Victorians showed itself in advertisements for 'medieval' and 'Tudor' inkstands. The humble user of ink probably contented himself with the glass bottle in which the ink was purchased or one of the very simple metal or glass inkpots sold by all stationers. Further down the scale the school child used a china inkwell, with or without a swivel lid of cheap metal to prevent dust affecting the ink. While the grander and more valuable items can be seen in museums or country houses, it is the smaller humbler versions, as with other writing accessories, that require the collector's keenest search.

Before leaving the inkpot and its associates, there is another important aspect of ink containers to be considered. Before the introduction of the fountain pen every writer needed ready access to an ink supply and this was equally true whether the user was static or travelling. If you were on the move from place to place you took your ink supply with you. Hence the importance of the portable writing set and the travelling inkstand. Portable forms of inkpot and quill holder go back a long way. Like many such utilitarian objects, the earliest ones were those in everyday use among humble people and

An engraved brass case for pen, ink, and sealing wax. It is inscribed 'Virgo me fecit in Sheffeild (sic) 1652' and on the bottom is a seal engraved with a coat of arms; the crowned head engraved on the hinge is possibly that of Charles I. Victoria & Albert Museum, London (M. 201-1914)

which have not survived. The medieval period made use of composite holders, in which a tiny supply of ink and some quills could be carried together hung from the scribe's belt (see page 88). The invaluable pen knife was also sometimes included, although as everyone needed to have a personal knife anyway, this was less frequently allowed for in early holders. The commonest material for these was some form of leather, though other materials such as metals were also used. When made for the nobility they were likely to be of silver or gold and to be lavishly decorated. A number of small portable writing sets, dating from the eighteenth century onward, survive. Made by the finest craftsmen of the day they are prized

collectors' pieces. Small enough to hold in the hand or fit in the pocket, they have changed considerably in shape from the kind that hung suspended from a strap or cord. The later kind were meant to stand on a surface, possibly a portable writing desk, though as we shall see this usually provided its own facilities. The small portable writing sets usually had one or two inkpots, all with (it was hoped) carefully secured lids, a small knife or blade for sharpening the quill, sometimes a seal, and a folding metal pen or small quill. It is in the travelling writing sets that the metal pen first becomes common, long before the commercial manufacture of the steel pen. Because this metal pen could be stored in several parts and fitted together when needed, the boxes could be made very small. For proper balance in writing a certain length of 'haft' is needed; once cut, the quill could not be joined together again, but with the metal pen it could be screwed or fitted to form the required length. Nevertheless, these early metal pens suffered from the disadvantages mentioned before, since they were liable to rust or corrode, and were not as flexible as the quill. So some portable writing sets included small quills (obviously the writer would endeavour to acquire some better ones if he faced a long spell of writing, which is why the portable writing sets often included a pen knife). These charming writing sets, so attractive to the collector, frequently look rather like snuff boxes from the outside, and as much attention and decoration was bestowed on them as on other similar trinkets.

We have so far been considering the more expensive pieces, but of course writing boxes were made for all purses and, therefore, in all materials. They all shared certain characteristics, being small composite containers, which were suitable for immediate use, though perhaps not for prolonged employment. The inkpots were meant to withstand considerable movement without leaking.

There were of course occasions when it was only necessary to have portable ink, and so even more numerous than writing sets are the portable inkpots which survive, especially from the nineteenth century.

Travelling inkpots of the period 1880–90. They are 'spring' inkpots, one with a patent secure fastening, the other with a double spring top. Both were covered in morocco leather.

When our ancestors travelled their journeys usually lasted very much longer than ours, and far greater preparation for them was required. Let us consider the Grand Tour, the 'finishing school' of the English nobility and near-nobility for nearly two centuries, until the Napoleonic wars caused its curtailment. Nearly every traveller, but especially those making the Grand Tour, was expected to send home long accounts of his experiences. Many also kept a travel diary – at least at the beginning of the tour. The traveller therefore needed to ensure that he took with him a portable writing set for immediate casual jotting, while a portable writing desk was probably stowed away among the mountain of baggage that accompanied him. His pens may have been kept separately, to be made or mended when required, and his portable inkpot was certainly an essential item. It is a pity that in descriptions of travels we hear only an occasional mention of these writing implements. But they were so much a part of the travellers' necessities that they were rarely considered worth reporting on unless they were unobtainable or went astray.

Even when the days of the Grand Tour had passed and been replaced by the Cook's Tour of the mid-nineteenth century, the absence of the fountain pen meant that to be sure of a supply of ink, the traveller still had to carry it with him, both at home and abroad. The Victorian period provided a great variety of travelling inkpots – guaranteed, or so it was hoped, not to leak in even the roughest sea. They were sealed in a variety of different ways. Sometimes there was simply a screw cap, though this was never very satisfactory. Other methods involved a stopper of cork or other material which might automatically be brought into place by means of a lever, and a lid (or even a double lid) which could be placed in position by means of a spring, screw or similar device. Such portable inkpots are still to be found and collectors may enjoy the variety of devices which have been invented for rendering them leak proof. Their use continued long after the invention of the fountain pen since this too needed to be refilled with ink from time to time. The portable writing set and inkpot have really only disappeared since the almost universal use of the ball-point pen. Even those devoted to the traditional form of nib are forced to admit that for travelling purposes the ball-point really has no rival. What inkpot, however capacious, can compete with a pen which offers miles of writing in its small interior?

In pictures of the medieval scribe at work, he is usually shown seated before a sloping 'desk'. This desk is often apparently no more than a type of lectern. It gradually became obvious that it would be useful to have books stored to hand, as well as to have writing implements fixed in various places near to the writer. But as an article of furniture in the homes of non-professional writers, the desk (or later the bureau) was slow in making its appearance. The amount of furniture in any room up to the early nineteenth century was far less than we are accustomed to. Instead of a desk it was more common to have a writing box, which could be placed on a suitable surface, usually a table. Some of these early boxes were most elaborate – the one in the Victoria and Albert Museum said to have belonged to Henry VIII is of painted and gilded leather. Others might be of carved oak, walnut or other woods, and frequently decorated with ivory or other inlays. It was from the combination of the sloping-topped writing box and the table that writing bureaux and desks

Day's patent revolving-top inkstand, as exhibited at the 1862 International Exhibition. The makers criticised existing forms of portable inkstands, saying that their mechanism easily became out of order. Day's inkstand, it was claimed, could not corrode and was guaranteed to retain the ink securely in whatever way it might be carried. It worked on the same principle 'by which the bayonet is affixed to the Enfield rifle'.

Dating from about 1525, this desk is covered with painted and gilt leather, decorated with the royal arms and heraldic badges of Henry VIII and Catherine of Aragon, and the figures of Mars and Venus. Victoria & Albert Museum, London (W. 29-1932)

eventually evolved, but in this chapter we are more concerned with the portable or travelling desk and writing box, since these are objects the collector can hope to acquire for himself.

Like the traveller on the Grand Tour, anyone making a prolonged stay away from home also tended to take his own portable writing desk with him. And many visits *were* prolonged in the eighteenth and nineteenth centuries, when travelling and communications were less speedy than today. As we read in novels such as those by Jane Austen, visits tended to last for weeks at least, and often longer. Diaries and memoirs, especially those of the upper classes, show people on almost continual rounds of visits. Although hosts would have frequently provided a certain amount of writing material for their guests, many people liked to take their own equipment with them. Such portable or travelling writing desks or boxes varied as much as other writing implements. Even today when they are found bereft of most of their fitments, they can usually be distinguished from other boxes which they resemble externally, by the fact that the lid, when opened, forms a sloping surface similar to that of a desk. When in this position ready to be used as a writing surface, the place for inkpots, pens, and other equipment lies at the top, while both parts of the writing 'table' are usually meant to act as covers to the storage space for stationery or other items below. Sometimes a drawer has been added on one side, concealed, in the case of larger boxes, by the handles and which can only be opened when the main desk has been unlocked.

These boxes were for the grand journeys, and long stays, and especially for people who travelled in their own carriages. But what of the less affluent traveller, especially when the extension of the railway system

'Gentlemen's writing desks' could be bought in walnut, mahogany, or rosewood. They were fully fitted and lined, and some had side handles for carrying. Most of them had brass corners, and some had a further strengthening of brass bands or edges. This type was common throughout the Victorian period, although some are of an even earlier date.

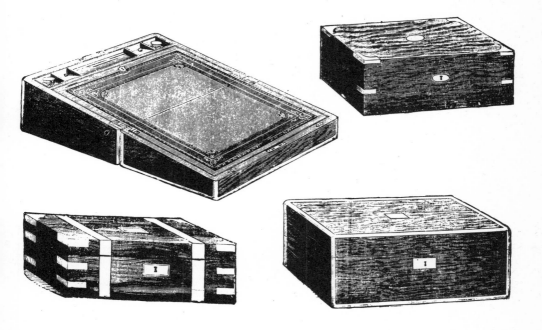

Two late nineteenth-century papier mâché writing desks. The top one was described as 'writing desk, "camp", with two cut bottles, and a velvet lined writing slope, stationery rack, and stamp box, with painted birds and flowers on a grey or silvered ground'. The lower one, a writing desk and inkstand combined, had crystal ink bottles with gilt mounts and a wafer box, and the writing surface was covered in blue or crimson silk velvet.

led to greater mobility and shorter stays? For them a simpler form of writing compendium was offered – the writing case. This presupposed that a writing surface of some sort would always be available. Less solid than the writing box, it was usually made of leather. 'Was' is perhaps hardly the word, since this item, though no longer so popular, is still with us and is often given as a birthday present or travelling gift. Nowadays it probably contains space for a writing pad and envelopes, some pens, and a pencil and little more. It is merely a way of keeping all the essentials for writing a letter together in one, easily findable place. But the earlier writing cases had to find space for much more: pens certainly, but also nibs, blotting paper, *sheets* of notepaper rather than writing pads, envelopes, and also later in the nineteenth century, until quite recently, postcards. There

A 'tourist writing case' of French morocco leather, lined with leather and satin. Made about 1880 it held various sizes of notepaper and envelopes, together with pens, pencil, paperknife, etc.

was perhaps a space for stamps and in earlier ones for wafers. Some even included one of the small travelling inkpots mentioned earlier. But the whole case was much smaller and more portable than the older writing box, which, though it might *accompany* the traveller, could never be packed in the portmanteau or suitcase as the writing case could be.

Today we have almost solved the container problem. If ink is needed, it is bought in bottles and rarely decanted into anything more elegant. The

A writing desk exhibited by Asprey's of Bond Street, London, at the 1862 exhibition. It was described in the catalogue as 'an Adelaide writing desk in Coromandel wood with pierced gilt and engraved mounts, with china medallions and fitted with every requisite for correspondence'.

chances are that a ball-point pen is used, especially when travelling, and so the ink supply goes unobtrusively with us. We do not need pounce or blotting paper, nor do we need nibs. Our pen tucks into a pocket or handbag, and our writing paper and envelopes tend to be packed into our cases just like any other item. Our suitcase *may* have a special pocket in which we can place such things, or we may even possess a small writing case. More expensive items, including the elaborately fitted leather attaché case, can still be seen in shops today – but who buys them? And, more important in these days of air travel, who, having been given one of these heavy objects, actually takes it on his travels?

Typewriters

There can be few people other than professional
calligraphers who enjoy the labour of writing for its
own sake. Many a hard-pressed medieval copyist or
latter-day business man must have longed for something that would relieve him of the manual labour
inherent in his task of handwriting and copying. A
machine that would successfully accomplish this for
him must have seemed an impossible dream. Yet
today we accept the typewriter without so much as
a backward glance at its evolution. What was de-
manded of any potential mechanical writer? Obviously it needed to function more speedily than the
hand or there was no point in changing from
the older method. It also had to be simple to use,
efficient in the production of its finished work, quiet
in action, and reasonably inexpensive to acquire.
Although we might now consider the production of
multiple carbon copies to be an important feature
of the typewriter, this aspect was not a primary one
in the drive towards its development.

The typewriter as we know it originated from the
search for a method to enable blind people to read
and write by means of embossed letters. The ways

The type-bars of the Sholes and Glidden typewriter (1874–6) hang vertically and strike upward. This machine could be worked rapidly but printed in capital letters only. The ribbon lies horizontally across the top and the keyboard is similar to the modern or 'universal' keyboard. Science Museum, London (1881-55)

by which the modern machine evolved were as varied as those experiments with the fountain pen. As with the pen, it was a question of solving a number of problems simultaneously. Many patents, some fanciful, some practical, were applied for after the first one in 1714 commenced the history of the typewriter. This was the patent granted to Henry Mill 'for an artificial machine or method for the impressing or transcribing of letters singly or progressively one after another'. Unfortunately we have no further information concerning this early machine. But efforts to assist the blind continued, bringing nearer the evolution of the modern typewriter. The final step came from the development of a machine intended to number consecutively the pages of books. This was helped by the assimilation of technical knowledge gained from the many efforts that were going on to produce a mechanical method of writing. It was two Americans, Christopher Sholes and Carlos Glidden, who eventually produced a workable and potentially marketable model. This was shown to the small-arms manufacturers E. Remington & Sons in 1873 by their associate James Densmore, and in 1874 the first machine issued from the Remington factory.

By the 1880s commerce in many countries was ready for such an instrument. This had not been the case in the past and ideas had been allowed to lapse from lack of interest. Now the machine's potential was speedily appreciated, in spite of the fact that much work needed to be done before its mechanics were entirely satisfactory for all commercial purposes. As a result, the period between 1874 and the end of the century produced a great many variations both in the design of machines and in the solutions to the problems involved. The typewriter of today in fact bears a surprising resemblance to the first one produced by Sholes and Glidden, in spite of other ingenious instruments produced by later designers.

Many of the differences between late nineteenth-century versions and the modern typewriter concern the method of placing the type on the paper, the visibility (or otherwise) of that type on the paper, and the method of causing the paper (or the type) to progress. In the modern typewriter the type sits in a semi-circular 'basket' before the carriage and by depressing the keyboard, the appropriate piece of type strikes down upon a prepared ribbon. The paper is moved automatically as the keys are depressed. In some of the late nineteenth-century models, such as the 'Crandall' of 1893, the type, instead of being in a 'basket', was on a 'sleeve' which rotated. Other methods included a 'typewheel' as in the 'Columbia' of 1886. The 'Oliver' typewriter of 1894 was one of the few which offered a type-strike down from the side, allowing the operator to see the letter printed. This is something we tend to take for granted, but many earlier designers found it a considerable problem. In the end the generally used type-strike did not come from the back, side, or 'grasshopper movement', but from the front.

The inking of the type was another problem. Sometimes this was done by bringing the type into contact with inking pads or inking rollers, although eventually it was the ribbon which carried the day. Visibility of the typed work was important and some of the early models suffered from the fact that work already typed was hidden from the operator. But possibly more important was the need to arrange the keyboard in such a way that when used at speed the type bars would not tangle. Two main layouts of the keyboard were suggested: the 'universal' and the

The Crandall No 3 typewriter of 1893 was one of the type-sleeve class. The type-sleeve carried six rows of characters and was struck against the platen in the centre, so providing at least partially visible type. The curved arrangement of the keys and the decorative bodywork is distinctive. Science Museum, London (1934-644)

'ideal'. The 'ideal' had only a short life in the last decade of the nineteenth century, while the 'universal', often known as 'qwerty' from the arrangement of the first line, has continued as the usual form of keyboard arrangement. It is nevertheless an arbitrary arrangement and far from ideal. Attempts have frequently been made to change it, so far without success. Certainly a great deal of expense would be involved in retraining now that typewriters are so universally employed.

The national collection of typewriters is housed at

This Oliver typewriter No 1 of 1894 is an example of the 'down-strike-from-side' class. The type-bars are staggered in banks at each side and strike on to the platen in the centre, thus making the finished type completely visible. Science Museum, London (1936-31)

The Hammond 'Ideal' typewriter of 1884 was one of the many varieties of typewriter which moved away in shape from the more familiar Sholes and Glidden example. The impression is made by a hammer striking the paper against the type-selector. Science Museum, London (1931-281)

the Science Museum in London. The museum issues a very useful guide to the collection which goes into considerable detail over the various principals on which the early models were constructed. It is quite interesting to note how very strange some of the models look at a time when the Remington version was already in existence. Some, such as the Hammond 'Ideal' typewriter of 1884, had a semi-circular keyboard, while the 'Bar-Lock' typewriter of 1889 had an engaging piece of 'Art Nouveau' decoration on its metal front. As early as 1886 we find an advertisement for a portable typewriter, the 'Hall'. Its text reads remarkably like its modern counterpart, except that the rather flat-looking machine pictured in the advertisement reveals its period. Looking at all the early typewriters one is constantly impressed by the ingenious ways devised by their inventors to overcome the various technical problems involved, and also by the fine engineering of the machines themselves.

The typewriter also had a part to play which was quite outside the realm of technical development. The employment of a vast amount of female labour in its use greatly aided the emancipation of women and added another occupation to the previously very limited ones, such as governess, nurse, or maid servant. Answering the call of the typewriter, female clerks invaded the commercial and business world for the first time in large numbers during the closing decades of the nineteenth century. It is an interesting point that so faithful have they been to the instrument of their freedom that even today the word 'typist' conjures up an almost exclusively female form!

During the 1880s and 1890s a number of improvements were made in typewriter design including those which enabled touch typing to replace the sight system. Many of the new designs also allowed for the typed line to be fully visible to the operator. During this century many further refinements have been introduced and a certain amount of standardisation has taken place in the manufacture of typewriters. All now have the standard four-row keyboard and incorporate such things as tabulator keys, back-spacer, two-colour ribbon, stencil cutter and so on. But, as anyone who has had to buy a typewriter ribbon knows, there are still perhaps far too many different kinds of machines in production. With the increase in production and streamlining of methods, machines have become much cheaper. There is also a far wider range of portable typewriters available, so that they are now even within the reach of many students, if not yet of schoolchildren. Once it was not considered right to submit college essays in typed form, but now, no doubt to the relief of many tutors, it is positively encouraged. Typing ability is expected of people in many of the professions as well as in commerce and with the home typewriter easily available it is not so difficult to acquire – *good* typing ability is quite another matter!

The office typewriter having become neat, easily

(A) An advertisement for a Remington typewriter, showing the amount of detail considered necessary to sell the new 'writing machine'. From the 'Illustrated London News', vol 83 (1883). (B) By 30 October 1897, when this advertisement appeared in 'The Graphic', the typewriter had become more familiar, and this fact is reflected in the streamlining of the sales talk. (C) An advertisement for an early portable typewriter. From the 'Illustrated London News', vol 89 (1886).

handled, efficient, and reasonably priced, there followed the attempt to lighten the labour of mechanical writing even further by the development of the electric typewriter. But this, like a number of other lines branching off from the concept of the basic typewriter, belongs more to the field of technology and less to that of the potential collector.

We have briefly mentioned the duplicating ability of the typewriter and this aspect opens up another field, namely that of the stencil. The history of the search for a method, or methods, of duplicating the written or typed word form a separate subject, and one which has been fully dealt with elsewhere. Already the day of the typewriter carbon copy is passing with the advance of the copying machine. Even as its ability to duplicate was not a driving force in its development so today it has again become of less importance in the choice of the modern typewriter.

COLLECTING TYPEWRITERS

The mention of the decoration of the 'Bar-Lock' typewriter earlier, suggests one reason for collecting old typewriters, since they reflect the design standards of their period in the same way as other objects in daily use. Their decoration says as much about late Victorian and early Edwardian taste as their smoothly streamlined successor does about contemporary style. But the main interest in old typewriters, as in old fountain pens, lies in the development of the techniques which brought them to their present stage of evolution. To acquire a vintage typewriter, to find out how it worked, and then to repair and set it going again, may well appeal to the collector for whom the inkstand or pounce pot have no attraction. At the moment it is still possible to pick up typewriters dating from the beginning of this century although even these are rapidly disappearing into museums.

Just as in the 1880s no one would have considered collecting contemporary typewriters – for reasons of cost if for no other – so the same applies to the present models. For the private collector it will always be difficult to house many of these machines, of whatever date they may be, since even a portable typewriter is a bulky object. Nevertheless, the rescue and repair of one or two vintage machines, together with the excitement of the hunt for them in the first place, can prove a highly satisfying experience for the technically minded.

8 The Pencil

When we use the word 'pencil' we usually mean
the common black lead pencil in general use today.
Originally the word meant a brush, the tool used
by artists for painting. For drawing purposes the
artist would use either chalk or graphite in a
special holder. In the past the place of the pencil
in the modern child's life was largely taken
by the slate and the slate pencil. It was with
these tools that the child learnt to make his first
letters and on which he probably did his first
drawings. From the slate it was usual to progress to
writing with a quill pen and ink (or of course later
with a steel pen). Jottings which we now do with a
pencil were done on waxed writing tablets with a
metal stylus which leaves a track similar to that of a
pencil on paper. A stylus is still occasionally to be
found in eighteenth-century almanacks and note-
books, where it is for use on certain preliminary
blank pages of the notebook. The notebook was
coated so that the metal stylus leaves a track like
that of a pencil on paper.

It was the discovery of mines of pure graphite
in Cumberland during the reign of Elizabeth I
which led to the development of the pencil industry.
In *The Complete Book of Trades* (1843) we read
under 'Pencil maker':

116

The smaller size hair-brushes used by Painters obtain the term *pencil*; but those we have now in view are made of wood, having a groove into which black-lead is introduced. The lead itself, or plumbago, is a dark shining mineral, found on the Malvern hills, and in Cumberland; whence great quantities reach London; and the latter produce is sold by monthly exhibition, or vent, from the depôt underneath the chapel, in Essex-street, at various prices. Its value is regulated by its evenness and solidity, qualities which are bettered by age, and which some makers extend to indefinite periods. Formerly, Mr. John Middleton was the most celebrated maker in this respect; but at present Messrs. Brookman and Langdon manufacture the most desirable surveyors' pencils; and these necessarily command astonishingly high prices. Needless, perhaps, would be the task of pointing out the numerous impositions that are daily practised upon the public in this very necessary article; rank deceptions, which are also sought to be carried further home, by affixing to them the most respectable names – forged. A pencil of a penny price, and another value a shilling, have frequently the same appearance, externally.

The application of mechanical methods during the nineteenth century brought about a big revolution in the manufacture of pencils. By the time of the 1851 Exhibition the small town of Keswick in Cumberland was established as the centre of the pencil trade. Here the graphite or black lead was treated and sorted according to its varying quality of hardness. The Keswick manufacturers imported cedar wood needed for the outer case of the pencil from South America and made it up into suitably sized pieces.

For cheaper pencils the cedar wood was merely varnished – a process developed in the mid-nineteenth century which solved the problem of how to keep the 'stick' clean – and an impression of the manufacturer's name stamped on it. For better quality pencils the lettering was done in gold or silver and the wood of the pencil coloured. When all the processes of cutting, rounding, and lettering were completed, the pencils were packed in colourful boxes and despatched to the stationer. This process

FIG. 3.—ROUNDING PENCILS.

FIG. 4.—GILDING PENCILS.

FIG. 5.—MACHINE FOR CUTTING THE ENDS OF PENCILS.

FIG. 6.—POLISHING PENCILS.

Some of the stages in the manufacture of lead pencils as illustrated in an article 'Pencil Making at Keswick', which appeared in the 'Illustrated Magazine of Art', vol 2 (1854).

has not changed very much for more than a century, and beyond the manufacturer's name there is little to assist a collector with the dating of a particular pencil.

THE PROPELLING PENCIL

The desire to have a writing implement ready for immediate use gave rise to the development of the propelling pencil. Graphite is a very fragile material and needs careful protection. It is also very soft and liable to leave traces on anyone or anything coming into contact with it. In order to overcome these problems manufacturers made a variety of decorative cases to protect the graphite. Some propelling pencils were very simple. A slim

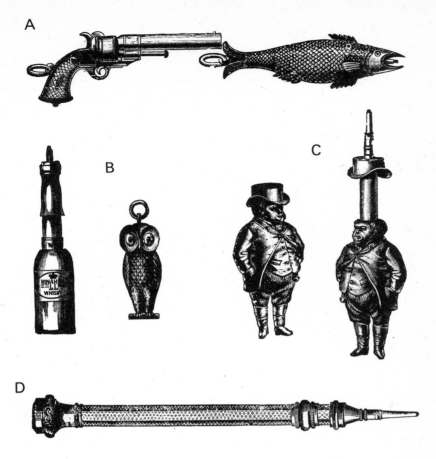

A

B

C

D

piece of lead was enclosed in a metal or ivory case. A clip on the outside of the case turned round a deeply incised spiral which pushed the lead down until enough of the point was projected for it to be used for writing. The lead could be retracted in the same way. In the more complicated versions of this technique the intricate workings were contained inside the case and in order to make the lead appear, some part of the holder had to be turned or pushed. Extra supplies of lead were at first sold in special little glass containers about six to a packet. Later a space in which to keep the refills was made at the top of the pencil. An india rubber was sometimes stuck on top of the pencil and the writer provided with everything he needed.

Some pen manufacturers were also makers of

(A, B, C) A great variety of fancy pencils became available in the late Victorian period. Among the luxury items were those illustrated, made in silver or gold by Sampson Morden. The whisky bottle and John Bull are shown opened out ready for writing. (D) A typical propelling pencil from the last quarter of the nineteenth century. This one was made of aluminium and contained a reserve of leads. It had a stone top and a sliding action to make the lead appear.

matching propelling pencils. These were handsomely boxed and sometimes, like the fountain pen, provided with a clip for the jacket pocket. For many years the pen and pencil set was considered an ideal gift.

COLLECTING PENCILS AND PROPELLING PENCILS

For the collector, most of the interest and excitement is in finding propelling pencils which were made for the novelty trade. Some were intended to be hung on a châtelaine or watch-chain at the waist; some were merely expensive trinkets. Whatever their intended use they are attractive objects and are now quite difficult to find. Many an uninteresting piece of black metal, lumped in a miscellaneous tray as an unidentifiable object, has revealed its content to a knowledgeable collector. Cleaned and renovated, it is found to be one of these attractive little pencils. The cheaper novelty pencils were in many cases made for children, and like so many 'toy' or novelty items they could never have been of much practical use. Into the 'toy' category come the giant-sized pencils, pencils in the form of an umbrella or a soldier, seaside souvenirs, manufacturers' advertisements, and fairings. Associated with such children's possessions is the school pencil box or pencil case. Not a beautiful object, but simply made of wood or other cheap material, in which the child could keep his pens, nibs, pencils, rubbers and other classroom necessities. These too can be found in various shapes and collected.

The hunt for early pencils and the search for variety is perhaps the most interesting aspect of collecting pencils. The more elaborate ones made in gold or silver by the firm of Sampson Morden, from about the 1830s, are rather more like jewellery than practical objects. Part of the charm of collecting early propelling pencils is that your blackened goose may turn out to be a silver – or even a golden – swan.

OPPOSITE
An early advertisement for a propelling pencil, from Pigot & Co's 'Metropolitan New Alphabetical Directory for 1827'.

𝕷𝖊𝖙𝖙𝖊𝖗𝖘   𝕻𝖆𝖙𝖊𝖓𝖙.

S. MORDAN & Co's
PATENT EVER-POINTED
PENCILS,

ARE upon a principle entirely new, and which combines utility with simplicity of construction. The Black Lead is not inclosed in wood, as usual, but in a SMALL Silver Tube, to which there is attached a mechanical contrivance for propelling the Lead as it is worn. The diameter of the Black Lead is so nicely proportioned as NOT TO REQUIRE EVER TO BE CUT OR POINTED, either for fine Writing, Outline, or Shading. The Cases for the Drawing Table or Writing Desk are of Ebony, Ivory, &c. ; and for the Pocket, there are Silver or Gold Sliding Cases, varying in taste and elegance. The Black Lead is of the finest quality, and prepared (by an entirely new chemical process) of five distinct degrees of hardness, and contained in boxes properly lettered for Artists, &c. and at the same time is perfectly suitable for all the purposes of business.

Milled Edges.   .. .. The Case .. ..

The Patentees desire to remark, that "*S. MORDAN & CO.'S PATENT*," is stamped on each of their Patent Pencils ; an attention to which, on the part of purchasers, will tend to check any attempt at imposition.

DIRECTIONS FOR USE.

Hold the two milled edges between the finger and thumb of the left hand. Turn the case with the other hand to the right, and the lead will be propelled as it is required for use ; but if, in exhibiting the case, or accidentally, the lead should be propelled too far out, turn the case the reverse way, and press in the point ; which of course in practical use, will seldom or ever be required.

The Black Lead Points are of five distinct sizes, as well as of five degrees of hardness, and contained in boxes marked as follow :—

The   V H   (very hard)   is very small in size..Seldom required
The   H   (hard)   is small............Hard and black, for fine Drawing
The   M   (medium)   is of a medium size.. For general purposes
The   S   (soft)   is larger............Black for Shading
The   V S   (very soft)   is largest ....Very black, for deep Shading
    The Cases are respectively marked with a corresponding Letter.

Attempts have lately been made to impose upon the Public an imitation of their Patent, in which the Lead being attached to the propelling wire, for the useless purpose of drawing back the Lead it is therefore in constant danger of breaking, while in those recommended to the Public by the Patentees, the Lead may be propelled as required for use, without incurring the slightest risk of breaking.—"*MORDAN & CO.'s PATENT*" is stamped on each case, and no other Patent has been granted for Pencils. They may be had of most of the respectable JEWELLERS, SILVERSMITHS, CUTLERS, AND STATIONERS IN THE UNITED KINGDOM.

MANUFACTORY,
No. 22,
Castle Street, near Finsbury Square,
LONDON.

9 The Ball-point Pen

✦✦

The idea of a ball-pointed pen is not a new one as the illustration on page 51 indicates. But the principle on which the modern ball-point works is quite revolutionary when compared with the traditional type of pen, however operated. Patents for a type of ball-point pen were taken out in the nineteenth century and a commercial version produced in 1895. But the invention of the present style of pen was the work of two Hungarian brothers, Ladislao and Georg Biro who first applied for patents in 1938. On the outbreak of World War II they moved to the Argentine where a company was formed to perfect and produce their pen. Subsequently patent rights were acquired on licence in other countries.

In the United States the development was encouraged by defence experts who needed a pen that would not leak at high altitudes, with an ink that while not affected by climatic changes was quick-drying and yet could have a long life within the pen. The final form of the ball-point comes near to reaching all these requirements. As in all pens which provide a reservoir of ink, one of the greatest

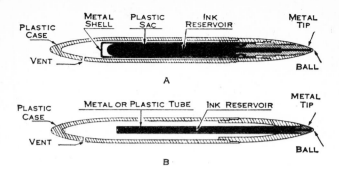

problems was to bring the ink supply to the point of writing in the correct amount when required, and without leaking when not in demand. 'Point' of writing is perhaps a misnomer in the ball-point pen since there is in fact no true point. The 'point' is a small tungsten carbide or steel ball-bearing which revolves within the barrel of the pen and is fed with ink by gravity or capillary action. This 'point' is virtually indestructible.

In its technique the action of the ball-point pen can be compared to the machine used for marking out tennis courts or football pitches. When the machine is pushed along a wheel revolves through a small container full of white liquid which it deposits as a white line. The ball at the end of the ball-point pen corresponds to the wheel. It rotates in the ink supply when the pen progresses over the paper and leaves an ink deposit. It is therefore very important to make sure that the ball will revolve smoothly. One of the disadvantages of the cheaper ball-point pens is that they occasionally 'miss' the inking by failing to rotate evenly. For this reason most suppliers provide a piece of paper on which a new pen can be tested. Another fault in ball-points is the tendency of the ink to 'fuzz' at the point, leaving a larger deposit than necessary. This is due more to the composition of the ink than to the technique involved in the manufacture of the pen.

It was discovered that a different kind of ink was necessary for the best results. This was developed by an Austrian chemist, Fran Seech, who produced

123

Highly prized by collectors, this beautiful millefiori paper-weight is French, probably Baccarat, from the mid-nineteenth century. The flower heads displayed through the glass are particularly decorative. Victoria & Albert Museum, London (4474c-1901)

a new type of ink based on glycol as a solvent. It is very different from the kind we are accustomed to buy in bottles and comes much nearer to the ink used for printing. It dries rapidly and needs no blotting paper. However, this does not mean that it no longer smudges in exercise books or gets on to small fingers. It does, and it then needs a considerable amount of effort to remove it. It is particularly difficult to remove from clothes.

The ball-point pen is produced by a number of different companies and comes with various refinements, or with none at all. It is particularly suitable for manufacture in modern materials and can be

mass produced and marketed very cheaply. Four ink colours are available: red, black, blue, and green, and the ink supply is remarkably long-lasting – Parker ball-points are said by their makers to offer 5 miles of writing. Some of the very cheap models are disposable. Once the ink is used up the whole pen is thrown away. Others are provided with refills and with retractable points which prevent any possibility of ink leakage. At the other end of the scale are ball-points sheathed in gold cases and made with all the glamour formerly associated with the more expensive fountain pens.

COLLECTING BALL-POINT PENS

It is difficult for the collector to know where to start: here is an item used by everybody and treasured by few. But to anyone studying the evo-lution of the ball-point over even a decade it will be obvious that there have been changes, both in style and mechanism. The collector of ball-point pens will have to scour the market as if he were searching for an antique as the various models are discarded and become obsolete very quickly. The hunt is none the less interesting for that.

An even newer form of writing implement is the felt-tip pen or pencil which is really a 'writing brush'. The present nature of the felt-tip's rapidly evaporating ink supply makes it unlikely to replace the ball-point, which for many people seems to be the final fulfilment of the pen maker's dream – the perfect ever-ready pen. But its effect on modern handwriting from which it has taken all character, that is another story!

10 Miscellaneous Writing Accessories

The miscellanea of writing accessories provide a number of interesting subjects for the collector. Looking round museums, or at the well-laid-out desk equipment of country houses, one becomes aware of various small objects, which, although not essential for writing purposes, obviously proved themselves both attractive and useful to the writer. Among such items may be included paperweights, paperknives, blotting pads or hand blotters, pen rests, pen wipers and stationery holders. If we go further and consider the office or school equipment of the past, it is possible to find even more objects worth collecting, though since these were primarily designed for utilitarian purposes they are rarely aesthetically satisfying. Into this last category come such things as clips for holding either large or small collections of paper, rubber stamps and stamp pads, and other such office items on the one hand, and slates, slate pencils, pencil boxes – and even fancy pencils – on the other. The selective collector will no doubt set a period or a more clearly defined subject limit to the objects he chooses to acquire. Others, especially at the beginning, may happily take whatever comes their way. All categories contain items which unless collected now will soon vanish forever, discarded in favour of newer and better instruments.

The paperweight can perhaps be considered the most beautiful of writing accessories, small and easy to store and attractive to display; the glass variety, in particular, has long been considered a desirable object. Fine examples fetch many thousands of pounds when they appear on the market. But there are plenty available for less wealthy collectors, especially for those who wish to acquire one or two merely as examples of desk furniture. The cheaper ones may be made of glass too, but without the elaboration of the grander collector's piece. They may be simple fairings or souvenirs from watering places; they can come in the form of animals, or as little more than stones picked up on the beach. More outré ones also turn up from time to time, such as one made from the hoof of a stag shot by some long-dead hunter. The choice is the collector's but at least paperweights remain among the items which can still have a practical use today, as well as being decorative objects in their own right.

Paperknives are also varied and interesting to collect and are still useful today. There are many people who prefer to open envelopes with a paperknife rather than use a table knife or tear roughly at the paper with their hands. A medieval scribe had little use for paperknives. His book or codex, made up of vellum leaves, came to him in foldings more or less ready in book form, save for the final trimming by the binder. But with the invention of printing it was realised that a larger number of pages could be printed together, provided they were imposed in the correct order. If you should chance to come across an unbound book and spread out the pages of one whole gathering (usually sixteen or thirty-two pages) you would find that in the resulting large square of paper, the pages appear in a very strange order. However, when this sheet is folded into a small booklet, the type appears on the front and back of the page in the correct order, but uncut along either the upper or side edges. In binding, these joins are

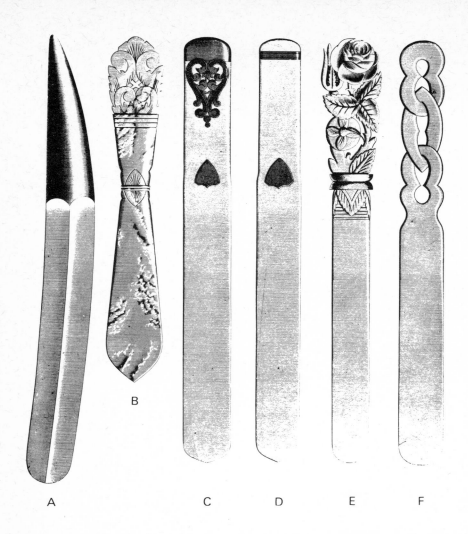

A   B   C   D   E   F

A selection of paperknives available in the last quarter of the nineteenth century: (a) ivory, with natural tusk handle; (b) pearl, with a carved and pierced handle; (c) ivory, with silver mounts; (d) ivory, with a mounted silver band and shield; (e) ivory, 'of stout quality', with a superior carved handle; (f) ivory, with a carved handle

usually shaved off and the resulting book opens easily at all pages. But everyone at some time has come across the book where a few pages have been missed, and a knife has been needed to slit them open. Nowadays we are used to having our books ready bound but the publishers' binding is little more than one hundred years old. Before it was customary for the purchaser or the bookseller to have the books bound. So a paperknife would have been a useful piece of equipment for the reader of such books. It was of course equally useful in reducing any sheet of paper to a desirable size. With the introduction of envelopes, the paperknife found a new and lasting use. Paperknives like other writing accessories can come in a variety of materials, the most suitable of which, in view of their smoothness, have always been ivory and mother-of-pearl. Paperknives made in ivory appear with all sorts of decoration, from the carved head of the Duke of Wellington to a Swiss edelweiss.

Containers for stationery have always been of importance and provision was frequently made for storing paper and envelopes in writing boxes or desks. In the same way bureaux also provided compartments for stationery. The stationery holder, however, was one of those charming inessential articles which the Victorians particularly enjoyed and there are some very attractive nineteenth-century examples to be found. The essential feature of a stationery holder was simple: adequate provision for paper and envelopes, which was stored in such a way as to be easily removed when needed by the writer. Within this basic requirement all variations were possible. The stationery box lent itself to much elaborate decoration. It can be found made of wood, perhaps carved with a gothic design; in deeply cut bog wood;

(a) A matching set of cases for envelopes and blotter dating from the late nineteenth century. This one, in coromandel wood, ornamented with nickel mounts, and lined with silk, was expensive. Cheaper versions were in walnut. (b) The 'Union' inkstand and envelope case combined. Made about 1865–70 it had glass inkpots, pen hollow, and drawer. (c) The 'New registered stationery cabinet' was made in oak or mahogany towards the end of the nineteenth century. It had spaces for holding all the necessary writing materials, three china inkwells, a glass pen tray, a long drawer at the bottom, and a revolving shutter to cover the rack.

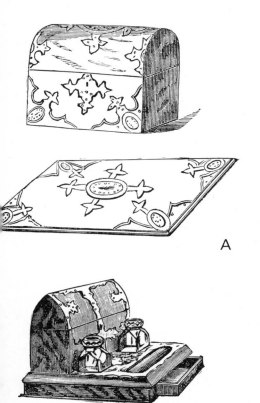

A

C

B

(a) Hand-painted floral blotting cases were popular in the late nineteenth century. Some were very elaborate like the Japanese style one on the right with inlaid mother-of-pearl and a velvet back; the one on the left has assorted flowers.
(b) A blotting book with 'superior' oleograph illustration, and another on the right made of French morocco leather with four nickelled corner mounts and centre ornament (c 1880–90)

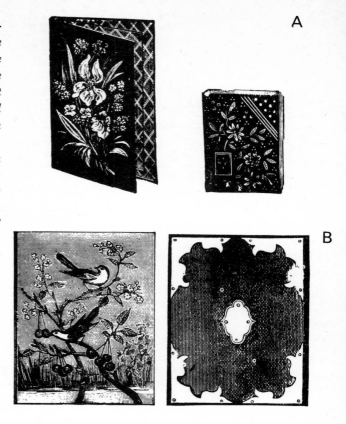

in the papier-mâché so much loved by the Victorians, especially when painted or inlaid; and in tooled leather. It was sometimes made to match the blotter, an item variously known as a blotting book, blotting case, or blotting pad, according to its precise function. In addition to the flat blotter there were – indeed still are – 'hand' blotters, which instead of being laid under the writing are curved like the base of a rocking horse and have a handle by which they are 'rocked' over the wet writing. Comparatively speaking, all blotting accessories have had a short life. They appeared only in the nineteenth century and have now almost disappeared, rendered unnecessary by the increasing use of ball-point pens. But they were decorative objects and frequently formed part of complete 'desk sets', though the collector would be lucky to find all such matching pieces still together.

A pen rest was usually incorporated with the ink-pot or inkstand. Sometimes this was merely a simple groove in front of the inkpots, but the disadvantage of this system was that any ink remaining on the nib could transfer itself to the groove and, possibly, on to another penholder. Such grooves were often painted or otherwise blackened to conceal this unsightly deposit of ink. A more satisfactory method was to provide a rack for the pens when not in use, either as part of the inkstand, or as a separate item. Racks, usually made of metal or wood, were decorated according to the prevailing taste of the day. Another method of storing pens was to place them upright in holes provided, usually around a central inkpot. This was more often the case with quill pens, whose nibs needed frequent mending anyway so that placing them straight down on the point was less disastrous. For steel nibs this method of storage was very unsatisfactory. Not only did it encourage ink to accumulate on the nib and risk increased corrosion,

A butterfly-shaped pen wiper made 'a very acceptable gift for Papa or Mama' in the Victorian era. From 'The Girl's Own Toy Maker and Book of Recreation' by E. and A. Landells (1860)

PEN-WIPERS.

Butterfly Pen-Wiper. These are very convenient and necessary additions to a writing-table; they are made in a great variety of ways, both plain and ornamental. The butterfly shape is easily made, and looks extremely pretty. First cut out of a piece of black velvet the shape of the butterfly, wings, &c.; button-hole-stitch all round the outside of the wings with yellow sewing silk as in the pattern; chain-stitch the inside markings. For the wings use red sewing silk, and fasten on small brass beads according to the figure. For the body of the butterfly cut out another

piece of black velvet the size you require, sew it up and stuff the inside with cotton wool; twist round the neck a piece of red sewing silk, cross the same over the back and again round the end, fasten it off, putting two beads in the head for the eyes. The inside leaves must be made of two or three pieces of black cloth, and another piece of plain velvet for the under covering; then stitch the body and the various parts together.

Commoner pen-wipers may be made of circular pieces of black velvet, neatly bound and sewed together in the middle, with two or three pieces of black cloth between them. Others again may be made altogether of black cloth, with small bright-coloured round pieces, about the size of a wafer, laid one over the other, like the scales of a fish.

Another method is to cut three pointed pieces of broad-cloth, about four inches long; each one must be stitched up separately, then turned wrong side outward. After they are made, the three are joined together at the seams, and a neat little bow is placed on the top. The bottom may either be bound or embroidered with fancy colours, but the insides must always be made of black flannel or cloth, as any other colours would soon be spoiled with the ink.

but if the nib rested too long on its point it was ruined and had to be replaced by another. It was therefore more common for steel pens to be shelved flat rather than upright, and even school desks provided this facility for pens and pencils. However, it is more common to store ball-points, when not in use, in the upright position, in containers which are specifically made in this style for them.

The risk of nib corrosion was somewhat lessened by the use of a pen wiper. This too had a fairly short life, although it survived into the present century. Both ink manufacturers and steel pen makers emphasised the need to wipe the nib clean after use, and some inkstands were even equipped with a special brush or piece of material for this purpose. But the pen wiper was an item which was especially well supplied by children lovingly making their first presents. Details for making them are to be found in works like *The Girl's Own Toy Maker and Book of Recreation* by E. and A. Landells (2nd ed 1860). Although such items were soon worn out or otherwise destroyed, occasionally they may still be found, nestling soft and inky in an old writing box.

Letter scales are items which span both business and private use and can also be an attractive object to collect. This piece of equipment is still not entirely outmoded, nor will it be as long as the cost of sending a letter is dependent on weight. This is no new regulation. Since the introduction of the penny post it has been possible, indeed in most cases compulsory, for postage to be paid in advance by means of stamps. Before that time it was the unlucky recipient who paid for the pleasure of receiving postal communications, even if they proved to be unwanted bills. The only exception to this was if the envelope had the signature or 'frank' of a peer of the realm or a member of Parliament. But payment was still by weight. It is for this reason that we often find old letters written in the ordinary way, and then continued *across* the existing writing as well. By this means the correspondent was saved the cost of additional sheets of paper – even if at the cost of eyesight and temper. It was therefore extremely useful, then as at all other times, to know the weight of a letter if in doubt of the likely charge for it. Letter scales can take a variety of forms, including the simple scale commonly used in post offices until recently, whereby the letter was weighed against small weights. There were also spring balances which were sometimes concealed in other pieces of equipment on the writing desk – they could pop out of a pencil or penholder for example. They can also be found neatly contained in their own velvet-lined box. Since they have never been superseded in the way that other desk items have been, and are still of use today, letter scales are not so easily found. They are nevertheless a delight to have, especially when cleaned to their original state. Delicately made and often of polished brass, perhaps also accompanied by a series of decreasingly small weights, they form a useful addition to even the most up-to-date desk.

Many varieties of writing implements and accessories have been briefly described in this survey. The scope for the collector, whatever the length of his purse, is considerable, though a lot of material even among yesterday's objects is fast disappearing. But there is still a chance to make new discoveries and to add further paragraphs to the history of these fascinating and useful items of man's social intercourse and economic development.

89
A nickel-plated sliding bar letter balance, showing the current postal rates (c 1870–80)

Postscript:
Where to find
and How to Study

❧❧❧❧❧❧❧❧❧❧❧❧❧❧❧❧❧❧❧❧❧❧❧❧❧❧❧❧❧

In going through this book the interested reader will already have noticed various references to sources of study and to collections of writing implements and accessories. This postscript is intended to bring together these scattered items of information. The obvious place in which to study many of the objects is a museum. The great national museums, in any country, will provide examples of inkstands and other accessories, especially those made of precious or semi-precious materials, or created by noted craftsmen. But smaller museums are also important in this field. For here it is possible to see the simpler objects and everyday items which do not come within the province of national collections. A local museum may well offer examples of the kind a collector may reasonably hope to acquire for himself, and whose preservation might otherwise have been neglected. So if you cannot visit one of the larger museums, such as the Victoria and Albert Museum in London, remember that your local museum may be more useful from a collecting point of view than one which shows only the very best items of this kind. Country houses,

such as those owned by the National Trust, often display a great variety of writing equipment used by former owners on desks and tables in rooms now open to the public. There is an increasing interest in the everyday objects used by people in the past, and museums frequently endeavour to portray typical rooms or shops of their own area: the York Museum is an example of one that does this, and the London Museum at present in Kensington Palace also has a 'shop' showing the contents of a stationers, with all the various items displayed for study in the 'window'.

But apart from visiting museums and country houses to look at actual examples of writing equipment and accessories, there is another method of study. This is not from the objects themselves but from representations of them. Obviously the

Children at work in early nine-teenth-century France, showing inkpot, pounce pot, pen knife, scissors, and quill. Also in use is a slate and a sponge (for erasure), which together with a slate pencil (not visible) were the tools for the beginner in writing. From T. P. Bertin's 'Le passe-temps de l'enfance; ou, le premier livre élémentaire' (1810)

enquiring collector will look carefully at the books listed in the bibliography on page   , choosing those which cover the particular objects in which he is especially interested. The study of writing implements can be carried even further. A picture gallery is a particularly fruitful source of information. In the National Gallery in London, or in Washington for that matter, there are many paintings which incorporate writing accessories of one sort or another. If it is not possible to visit the galleries in person, there are a number of books which provide adequate reproductions of the well-known collections. To study contemporary paintings is most valuable, as has been seen in the sections on medieval writing implements. Looking carefully it is surprising to see how many quite familiar paintings, especially portraits, have included an item or two of interest. In the field of portraiture it is not even necessary to have access to any well-known collections, since a small gallery may well include portraits of local worthies showing them posed pen in hand. A careful study of church monuments may also occasionally provide illustrations of contemporary pens or inkstands.

In this way by seeking information on the widest scale and not just from obvious sources, the collector can be constantly enlarging his acquaintance with the incredible variety of objects, from many periods and of various materials, which all come under the general heading of 'writing implements and accessories'.

Bibliography

GENERAL WORKS

Chambers's Encyclopaedia

Collecting Antiques

Country Life

Diringer, D. *The Hand Produced Book* (1953)

Encyclopaedia Britannica

Encyclopédie; ou, Dictionnaire raisonné des sciences, des arts et des métiers (1751–80)

Fairbank, A. *A Book of Scripts* (2nd ed 1968)

Lamb, C. (ed). *The Calligrapher's Handbook* (1956)

Latham, J. *Victoriana* (1971)

Heal, Sir A. *English Writing Masters and Their Copy Books* (1931)

Johnston, E. *Writing & Illuminating & Calligraphy* (1906)

Kettle, D. W. *Pens, Ink, and Paper,* (Sette of Odd Volumes, X) (1885)

A New and Complete Dictionary of Arts and Sciences (1754–5)

Poese, B. 'Writing Adjuncts', *Antiques Journal* (April 1972)

Ure, A. *A Dictionary of Arts, Manufactures and Mines* (2nd ed 1840)

Whalley, J. I. *English Handwriting, 1553–1850* (1969)

Writing through the Centuries: The Bishop Collection of Writing Implements (Biro Pens Ltd exhibition catalogue 1951)

Wyllie, D. *Writing – Origins and Development* (film strip made in co-operation with Biro-Swan Ltd)

Yesterday's Shopping: The Army & Navy Stores Catalogue, 1907 (reprint 1969)

Any general book on silver, porcelain, treen, pewter, leather, etc, will also include some writing accessories.

THE QUILL PEN

For manuscript illustrations, see general works on medieval manuscripts such as D'Ancona, P. and Aeschlimann, E. *The Art of Illumination: An Anthology of Manuscripts from the Sixth to the Sixteenth Century* (1969). See also the works mentioned in the general bibliography by Heal, Fairbank, and Whalley.

THE STEEL PEN

Bore, H. *The Story of the Invention of Steel Pens, with a Description of the Manufacturing Processes by Which They Are Produced* (1890)

Bunce, J. T. and Timmins, S. *Joseph Gillot, 1799–1872: A Sketch of His Life* (c 1880)

Lindsey, G. 'Steel Pens', *British Manufacturing Industries* (1876)

Timmins, S. 'The Birmingham Steel Pen Trade', *The Resources, Products and Industrial History of Birmingham* (1866)

See also various trade catalogues, eg Silber & Fleming (1872–89); and international exhibition catalogues, eg illustrated catalogues of the 1851 and 1862 exhibitions. Information also to be had from Birmingham Public Library and British Pens Ltd.

THE PEN KNIFE

See works on the quill pen (above), and, for later versions. general works on the cutlery trade of Birmingham etc.

THE FOUNTAIN AND RESERVOIR PEN

Maginnis, J. P. 'Reservoir, Fountain and Stylographic Pens', *Journal of the Royal Society of Arts*, LIII (1905)

Information also to be obtained from manufacturers of current fountain pens.

CONTAINERS: INKSTANDS, POUNCE POTS ETC

Rivera, B. and T. *Inkstands & Inkwells: A Collector's Guide* (1973)

Illustrations and descriptions are included in general works on the various materials, eg gold and silversmiths' work, treen, pewter, porcelain etc. Also see trade catalogues, encyclopedias etc.

TYPEWRITERS

Adler, M. H. *The Writing Machine* (1973)
Pearsall, R. *Collecting Mechanical Antiques* (1973)
Richards, G. T. (revised by Church, W. E.). *The History and Development of Typewriters* (1964)

PENCILS

Lefebure, M. *Cumberland Heritage* (1969)
'Pencil Making at Keswick', *Illustrated Magazine of Art* (1854)

Information also to be found in encyclopedias, and from various current manufacturers.

BALL-POINT PENS

Encyclopaedia Britannica
'Ball-point Pen', Jewks, J., Sawers, D., and Stillerman, R. *The Sources of Invention* (2nd ed 1969)

MISCELLANEOUS ITEMS

Information is included in many of the works quoted above, especially trade catalogues and encyclopedias; for paperweights see Hollister, P., jun. *The Encyclopedia of Glass Paperweights* (1969).

Acknowledgments

In a work covering as wide a field as this one, information has been gathered from many sources over a number of years. In particular I should like to thank Mr Church of the Science Museum, London, and Mr Spencer of the London Museum for their assistance, also my colleagues in the Departments of Metalwork, Ceramics, and Furniture and Woodwork, in the Victoria and Albert Museum, London. I am also grateful to my friends, especially Miss Enid Bassom, who have called my attention to various items over the years, and to Miss Heather Child of the Society of Scribes and Illuminators, for many instructive conversations. The opportunity of seeing the remarkable collection of writing implements belonging to Mr William Bishop has also been much appreciated. Information on modern pens has been received from Biro Bic Ltd, British Pens Ltd, Mentmore Manufacturing Co Ltd, Osmiroid Pens, and the Parker Pen Co Ltd. I should also like to acknowledge the help received from Mr W. A. Taylor, City Librarian of Birmingham Public Libraries, where so much material relating to the nineteenth-century pen trade is stored.

Finally I would like to thank all those whose names are not mentioned here but who have assisted in any way during the preparation of this book, not forgetting my friends whose patience has been sorely tried during my preoccupation with the study of writing implements and accessories.

LINE ILLUSTRATIONS

The pictures for the line illustrations in the text are from books in the Library of the Victoria and Albert Museum, London, with the exception of those on pages which have been taken from *The Story of the Invention of Steel Pens*, in the Library of the Science Museum, London. The photographs for these illustrations have been taken by my colleagues Peter Macdonald and Stanley Eost, to whom I offer my thanks for their skilful work.

J.I.W.

Index